THE POWER IN THE ROOM

THE POWER IN THE ROOM

Radical Education Through Youth
Organizing and Employment

Jay M. Gillen

Beacon Press, Boston

BEACON PRESS
24 Farnsworth Street
Boston, Massachusetts
www.beacon.org

Beacon Press books
are published under the auspices of
the Unitarian Universalist Association of Congregations.

28 27 26 25   8 7 6 5 4 3 2

This book is printed on acid-free paper that meets the uncoated
paper ANSI/NISO specifications for permanence as revised in 1992.

Some names and other identifying characteristics of people mentioned
in this book have been changed to protect their identities.

Text design by Michael Starkman at Wilsted & Taylor

Library of Congress Cataloging-in-Publication Data

Names: Gillen, Jay, author.
Title: The power in the room : radical education through youth organizing and
    employment / Jay M. Gillen.
Description: Boston : Beacon Press, [2019] | Includes bibliographical
    references.
Identifiers: lccn 2019004256 (print) | lccn 2019022219 (ebook) | isbn
    9780807064542 (pbk. : alk. paper)
Subjects: lcsh: Baltimore Algebra Project. | African
    Americans—Education—Maryland—Baltimore | African
    Americans—Maryland—Baltimore—Social conditions—21st century. |
    Community education—Maryland—Baltimore. | Community and
    school—Maryland—Baltimore.
Classification: lcc lc2803.b35 g55 2019 (print) | lcc lc2803.b35 (ebook)
    | ddc 371.829/96073—dc23
lc record available at https://lccn.loc.gov/2019004256
lc ebook record available at https://lccn.loc.gov/2019022219

The authorized representative in the EU for product safety and compliance is Easy Access System
Europe 16879218, Mustamäe tee 50, 10621 Tallinn, Estonia: http://beacon.org/eu-contact

For Thomas Nikundiwe

Young people are the power in the room.

—Omo Moses

CONTENTS

FOREWORD

Meet Alex, CMG, Deonte, Leon, David, TS, Daysha, Jamie, Katherine Engleman, Alanis Brown, Mira, Salima, Crystal, Bryan, Sherrod, Ms. T, and LS.

Meet them in this book by Jay Gillen, a writer who, in the language of Toni Morrison, "is unsettling, calling into question, taking another deeper look . . . whose writing is trouble for the warmonger, the torturer, the corporate thief, the political hack, the corrupt justice system, and for a comatose public."

Importantly, he wrote this book in his own language: *"It is how I talk to myself about how the young people talk to themselves"*—these young people of the Baltimore Algebra Project (BAP) with whom he has lived and learned how they talk to themselves for the past three decades.

Reflect that Jay and BAP youth, again in Morrison's language, come together to respond to their "perception of chaos" by enacting Morrison's atypical third response to chaos: "Stillness: not passivity, dumbfoundedness, or paralytic fear, but art." The art of creating a life within an "earned insurgency":

> BAP youth "collectively take on the work of making better arrangements for their lives than other people have done so far."

BAP youth construct, with their lives, meaning in the face of chaos.

Morrison speaks of "certain kinds of trauma visited on people

---

Toni Morrison, "Peril," *The Source of Self-Regard* (New York: Penguin Random House, 2019), vii–ix.

[that] are so deep, so cruel, that unlike money, unlike vengeance, even unlike justice or rights, or the goodwill of others, only writers can translate and turn sorrow into meaning." Such is the gift of Jay's book, or, as Morrison says, "the necessity."

BOB MOSES

THE POWER IN THE ROOM

Organizing, Economics, and the African American Educational Tradition

I descend from a line of Jewish teachers who worked in Eastern Europe in the nineteenth and early twentieth centuries. Near Suwalki, now in Poland, they ran their own secular Jewish schools as modernists—both men and women—translating the new genre of science fiction, for example, from French into a reinvented Hebrew. Some of them were socialists, fighting for freedom from ethnic and economic oppression. Many, including my gentle grandfather, fled from intolerable circumstances. All were victims of Russian, Polish, and Christian persecution, and the Nazi Holocaust left not a single Jew alive in the places where my ancestors once lived.

I have been a teacher for more than thirty years in Baltimore, where most of our public schools are desegregated in name only. I have come to follow and collaborate with a line of African-ancestored teachers who embody a tradition that sustains hope and joy in extraordinarily difficult circumstances. These teachers, both in and out of schools, draw on centuries of educational practices within Black communities that center around an idea of dignity, an essential worthiness, from which freedom can be grown and nurtured despite the surrounding hate. Their practices feel familiar to me in the quality of their ethics and the connection they assert between the work of the mind and political justice. I imagine a common ethical source for all cultures emerging from our shared human origins in Africa.

Many of the elements of an African American philosophy of education are spelled out and documented by scholar-activists such as Theresa Perry, Vincent Harding, Vanessa Siddle Walker, Heather Williams, Russell Rickford, Charles Payne, Carol Strickland, and others:[1]

- Children must develop identities as people who do intellectual and knowledge work but without creating a false dichotomy between the work of the mind and the work of the hands and body. Intellectual and cultural celebration must be integrated into each child's personality as an ordinary part of their daily activities, and that integrated personality must be encouraged to find expression and usefulness through thinking, communicating, moving, and making.

- Both peer and intergenerational group contexts are important for developing identity. African American children and young people can and do create group identities around their intellectual and cultural brilliance. This must be affirmed by everyone around them.

- The historically dynamic achievement of African American educational institutions should be taught explicitly, so that young people come to see themselves as part of a sustained effort to imagine and help realize a more just world.

The teachers I learn from in this tradition see each child's life in their care as both unique and representative: unique in the sense that each individual human being deserves to learn and to thrive; and representative in the sense that no one can escape the judgments of the world—the tests, the confrontations, the suffering—and these teachers therefore long to read in each child's life, and in the lives of all the community's children, a story of overcoming, a story of survival and even of victory.

Thousands of teachers, artists, artisans, musicians, preachers, intellectuals, farmers, cooks, and poets have thought of themselves as raising Black children into adulthood so that those children could "lift every voice and sing," as the anthem urges. Sometimes they have started schools or churches, sometimes they have joined already-existing institutions to create the environment where children could both thrive in the present and also learn to cope with the shared human burden, especially heavy for African children in America, of carrying the past successfully into the future.

As with all human endeavors, this work of education is never smooth. The violence of America tries to obliterate Black cultural abundance. The cruelty of poverty or of patriarchy still blocks pathways to intellectual development. Illness constricts effort, but also ego, envy, fear, or simply misunderstandings and failures of generosity and empathy. Prominent, too, are the obstacles generated by personal success. Class divisions within oppressed communities are exacerbated and exploited by both the economics and the symbolism of White capitalist supremacy. These divisions often poison relations even between members of the same family, and class markers can end up taking on a life of their own.

But obstacles are not the end of the story. The ideas developed in this book try to advance strategies that have emerged and continue to exist right within the hollows and openings of American power. In particular, I try to reconnect three aspects of freedom work that have always been understood to go together but whose relation to each other has become confused and difficult to see. We tend to think of education as one thing, and we think of economics as something separate from education. In popular understanding, the connection between the two is that you need an education to get a job: the one comes first; the other comes after. But things are not so simple. And the relation between education and a third aspect, political action or organizing, is even more complex. In the African American liberatory tradition, education, economic strategies, and organizing for freedom must be developed all at once or not at all. They are in fact one topic, not three.

I teach nowadays in a women's jail in Maryland—a jail for young women, as young as eleven, as old as nineteen. Although African Americans make up only 30 percent of the state population, they are 77 percent of the jailed youth.[2]

"Not a jail!" the authorities insist. This is a "detention center." The girls are "detained," not "jailed." "Detention" as in a school detention for tardiness or playing hooky. And it is true that as many as 12 percent of girls in detention centers nationwide are charged with no crime at all.[3] They are foster children, wards of the state. They ran away from somewhere: from rules, or from beatings, or from rape, or from hunger. But the state has nowhere else to house them. No one wants them. So they are detained, which means (at my jail) handcuffed, shackled, brought to a compound, placed behind door after door of locked steel, surrounded by barbed wire, surveilled every second, clothed drearily and uniformly, shut off from all normal communications with friends, and drugged mightily to medicate their noncompliance. Many were charged once with a minor crime or for using or selling drugs but violated the conditions of their probation by missing school, or cursing at a teacher, or smoking, or drinking, and are locked up to remind them of their responsibilities to society. A small number have been charged with murder or carjacking or robbery.

Most of the adults who work with the girls are kind, thoughtful, worn-out, largely powerless employees of the state. Over 90 percent are African-ancestored. We do what we are told for the most part and try to ease the girls' burden a little in whatever ways we can. But even here, pushed to the bottom, the brilliance of young people finds its own way. There are many examples to choose from: poetry, debate, art, music, dance, mathematics—not all necessarily sanctioned by the institution.

How our culture came up with the idea of jails for girls and boys is a historical question that this book does not explore in detail. But here is a story about literacy and freedom and employment that shows how hard it is to stamp out the spark of longing for community and connection: Bedtime is difficult at the detention center. There are many emotions. The girls and the guards are both tired. A transition must be made from the relative openness of the dayroom, to the confinement of the bedrooms, which are designed, thankfully, more like dorm rooms than cells. Ms. T., a shift supervisor for the guards, is universally respected for her calm strength and wisdom. LS is only fourteen years old and charged with very serious crimes. The saint, Ms. T., waits every night till two or three in the morning when LS finally winds down enough to stop running and collapses on the floor outside her room, exhausted. The guards have tried many times to restrain LS forcibly, but these attempts often end up unproductive and dangerous, because LS fights back. In fact, anyone else may get their face scratched, but when she is finally tired enough to sleep, LS allows Ms. T. to wrestle her into bed.

To guard against acts or accusations of sexual assault, the only physical contact permitted in the institution is "restraint" when a young person refuses to comply with commands. But it is the physical contact of a living being that LS craves, and so she and Ms. T. have worked out wordlessly this permitted method. LS collapses and refuses to move. Ms. T. is then allowed to wrestle her lovingly into bed. Everyone is happy (at the price to Ms. T. of her aching back), and the surveillance cameras reveal an entirely legal instance of human contact, night after night. In bed, LS asks Ms. T. to read her once more the letter her father wrote last week, then falls asleep for a few hours until the next day's compulsions and refusals begin again. In a quiet moment, she will dictate a response to her father that one of her friends will lovingly write down.

I read the story this way: Ms. T. carries the wisdom of survival and of cherishing each child as a strategy to overcome injustice, not allowing the child to simply "get her way," but recognizing the infinite complexity of what the child needs. LS understands love and demands that she be loved; in the midst of impossibly difficult circumstances, she figures out how to be held by someone who loves her. The father's letter is crucial to connect what the state tries to sever: the connection between parents and children, between community and children—an imposed social disintegration that dates, of course, to the first kidnappings in Africa. And Ms. T., quintessentially a teacher, does whatever she can to hold together parents and children, community and children. She reads to the child and she answers the child's questions. Finally, LS does not accept her position as hopeless and without resources; she acts, and compels reactions from adults. She naturally turns to her peers for help. She asks them to share in writing a letter back to her father, trying to be close to him however she can. Her peers agree to help.

Everyone in the story has positive things that they want to do and accomplish, but most of their days are spent in frustration, since they are not permitted to do the things that will actually meet their needs. They are held idle, "unemployed" in the sense that their labor is not thought to be needed. This is, after all, one of the functions of jail as punishment; the convict is meant to feel useless. Sadly, for many young people in poverty, the experience of going to school feels very much the same as the uselessness of being locked up. In LS's story, literacy, employment (being needed for something, being useful), and freedom must be thought about all at once.

There are many arms available to hold young people through their troubles. And there are countless young people who are currently unemployed in many senses of the word but who could be lifting up each other's brilliance in knowledge work—creating, inventing, doing. But we have not yet developed a strategy for moving from local manifestations of this African American educational tradition to larger scale manifestations. This book is intended as a description of one approach to that problem, an approach that emphasizes the material, economic base for building educational and political institutions. This is by no means a new idea, but I hope to show how we can use novel aspects of our particular moment in history along with already-existing grassroots efforts to expand the traditions of education for liberation to many more practitioners around the country.

To round out this introduction, I would like to explain the concrete origins of the organization that has nurtured me for twenty-five years, the Baltimore Algebra Project (BAP). BAP took root in the national Algebra Project, which itself emerged from one particular current of the Black freedom struggle, the current that Ella Baker and the young people of the Student Nonviolent Coordinating Committee, or SNCC, helped to create. To understand these origins, we have to think a little more about the nature of work.

Nothing is more cruel than "unemployment," and the story

that begins with slavery must always in some sense be a story about "employment," jarring as it is to use that word in this context. Perversions of the idea of employment continue to affect African Americans to this day. Enslaved people were not "employed" but were compelled to work without compensation. Prisoners today are not "employed" but rather labor under a system of coercion for pennies an hour, if they are paid at all. The sharecropping and peonage systems treated labor not as employment but as the working off of debt always already incurred. The many African Americans who make ends meet through one hustle or another are not exactly "employed" in the hustle—they are surviving. And someone who wants to work full-time but finds their hours cut and cut again and who then "isn't needed" for a couple of weeks, months, or years at a time—they aren't exactly "employed" either. What about the Black man or woman with a college degree who can only find a retail or service job, not in their field? Are they "employed"?

We tell our children that they should do well in school so that they can get a job. But getting a job and earning a livelihood isn't that simple in White supremacist America. Black heroes have long known this and have always thought further than some simplistic concept of employment. For hundreds of years they have been developing economic ideas to create relationships that are essentially collaborative and collective instead of alienating and vulnerable. Rather than accept economic relations of subservience, they have invented alternative relations through which Black communities can support themselves economically and culturally despite the oppressive structures all around.

Economist Jessica Gordon Nembhard's important study *Collective Courage* chronicles and analyzes all kinds of cooperative economic strategies deployed by African Americans, including maroon encampments of fugitives, mutual aid societies, agricultural unions, Marcus Garvey's economic democracy, and many variations of formally structured consumer and producer co-ops.[4] All of these strategies rejected narrow conceptions of workers as free agents exchanging their labor for a fair wage in an open marketplace. The collectivist approaches to economic empowerment centered instead on creative structures for groups of people to organize resources, capital, and labor in pursuit of common goals.

Among many other key figures, Ella Baker stands out in Nembhard's book for the scope of her efforts in promoting new economic relationships within Black communities. Most importantly, Baker understood and articulated historically and culturally rooted connections between economic, political, and educational freedoms. In Baker's tradition of Black collectivism, it doesn't make sense to say that you need a good education *so that* you can get a good job. That kind of causal link was recognized long ago as much too simplistic. Being brilliant and accomplished is no guarantee at all that White people will make room for you in their economic or political systems. You need collective economic and political independence from White supremacy—or at least attitudes that prefigure that independence and the uprooting of White supremacy—*so that* education can contribute to liberation rather than to new forms of enslavement and subordination.

Baker's consciousness developed through the defiant collectivist self-determination of her parents and grandparents. Her maternal grandmother, daughter of a slave master, refused to marry the light-skinned person she was assigned to and later married a very dark-skinned man instead. As punishment, she was sent to work in the fields where, she later told her granddaughter, she would work all day but then dance defiantly all night.[5] Anna Baker, Ella's mother, "would have been very much at home leading a feminist movement," Ella told a biographer in the 1970s.[6] Anna organized material support of many different kinds for the wider Black community through women's associations within the Baptist church, and she pushed in the dangerous early decades of the twentieth century for economic and political freedoms without regard to White intimidation.[7]

These examples among others pointed Baker toward a practical philosophy that was grounded in economic self-sufficiency as a foundation for both political organization and for study. The Young Negroes' Cooperative League (YNCL), for example, was founded with Baker's help in 1930 to create cooperatives with hopes that they would lead eventually to a local bank and factories for producing clothes, household items, and food for Black communities. Although these dreams were not realized and the YNCL folded in 1936, Baker helped young people from scores of cities to conceptualize economic and social relations that put them in control of how they lived their lives. Equality for women was an explicit part of the YNCL program, and education was understood as fundamentally intertwined with cooperative economics.

In the early 1960s Ella Baker's student, Bob Moses, applied these lessons concretely in his work as Mississippi field secretary of the Student Nonviolent Coordinating Committee. SNCC had been formed in the summer of 1960 in response to a call Baker sent out for students involved in the sit-in movement to come together and organize on a national scale. But the students had not yet found a way to push civil rights organizing into the most dangerous parts of the deep South. Baker connected Moses to a network of contacts she had established in Mississippi, Alabama, and Louisiana—seasoned freedom fighters who could keep him and the other SNCC workers alive, partly because of the economic beachheads these contacts had already established: Amzie Moore owned a gas station; Aaron Henry was a pharmacist; both were members of the Fraternal Order of Friendship that supported low-cost medical care for Black people. Their economic footing and collectivist ideology made it possible for them to shield the young voting rights workers from the worst excesses of their White opponents. Nevertheless, White Mississippians used economic power against anyone over whom they had leverage. Sharecroppers and plantation workers were denied work or had food aid withheld if they tried to register to vote. Fannie Lou Hamer was thrown out of both her job and her home. The vital link between economic and political dependency or independence was lost on no one.

Moses's Mississippi work and subsequent career also reveals the nexus of politics and education. In 1963, Federal District Court judge Claude Clayton of Greenville, Mississippi, asked Moses, "Why are you taking these illiterates to register to vote?" And Moses responded that the judge "couldn't have his cake and eat it, too. You can't deny a whole segment of the population access to literacy because they have no political representation, and then turn around and deny them access to politics because they are illiterate."[8]

Freedom Summer in 1964 challenged White supremacy on all three fronts. The voter registration drive and Mississippi Freedom Democratic Party (MFDP) organized for political power. MFDP's platform was significantly about economic liberation, access to capital, eliminating employment discrimination, and job security. And the curriculum of the Freedom Schools was explicitly focused on Black liberation and grassroots literacy, beginning with the paradigmatic example of the Haitian Revolution.[9]

The work of SNCC—supported by locally entrenched veterans like Amzie Moore—succeeded in breaking open the political stranglehold to an extent, but SNCC did not succeed in abolishing or even damaging educational or economic apartheid. Consequently, the political gains of those years remain under threat, as can be seen from the recent evisceration of the Voting Rights Act by state governments with assistance from the US Supreme Court and Department of Justice.

The Algebra Project, founded by Moses in 1982, builds on the deeply rooted understanding in African American culture that these things go together: a degree of economic autonomy leading to political assertions and the concurrent development of a culturally centering educational philosophy. In the case of the Algebra Project, economic autonomy is associated with mastery of twenty-first-century abstract symbolic languages—math literacy—just as access to verbal literacy grounded the freedom struggles of the last century. Centered on mathematics classrooms and curriculum but extending into political organizing on a national scale involving young people, families, teachers, professional mathematicians, and professional organizers, the Algebra Project uses math literacy as an organizing tool to build a demand for first-class educational citizenship as a way to underwrite first-class political and economic citizenship.

I have worked as both a classroom mathematics teacher, using pedagogy developed over several decades by the Algebra Project, and also as an adult organizer and encourager of the youth-controlled

Baltimore Algebra Project. In this book I hope to pull together certain threads of educational practice that make use of the historical understanding described above and to show that many efforts already exist at the grassroots level that can be organized to help young people build a comprehensive national agenda for radical change. It is absurd that we hold people like LS and her peers in a state of inaction for months and years at a time and that we assign people like Ms. T. to pick up the pieces of the mess we have made, instead of employing their gifts to help create local institutions of strength and beauty. Not only in the jails but also in the schools, thousands upon thousands of young people and adults are vastly underemployed. We should use what we already know to rearrange a little capital and to finance a much more productive approach to teaching and learning. One way this goal might be accomplished is described in the chapters that follow.

PART I

STRUCTURES

CHAPTER 1

From Crawl Spaces
to a Youth Economy

A crazy walk. West Baltimore. Street lights out. Broken glass. Hollowed-out buildings. Now and then a teenager rides by on a kid's bike much too small for him, the quickest way to whatever hustle he has going on.

Alex, tall and handsome, walks home a couple of miles in the cold dark. The bus ticket that gets you home from school expired at six, but the meeting at the Algebra Project office ran till nine. He pushed hard at the meeting to increase the math tutors' wages by fifty cents an hour, so they would make the same as the organizers. But the organizers thought they deserved more, since they were expected to be out in the evenings and weekends when there were meetings or presentations at community forums, or if they were getting ready for a demonstration. The tutors only needed to stay after school an hour and a half, teach a little math, pass out some snacks, and get paid.

As he walks, Alex imagines nominating himself to become an organizer next year, when tenth grade starts. He could make a good speech. His friends would vote for him. He could still tutor after school, except Tuesdays and Thursdays when the organizers have their regular meetings. His mother and father might not like it, though. They are always telling him that even though he looks like an American and sounds like an American, he is Nigerian, and he needs to stay out of trouble. He smiles as he walks, imagining the speech he will give. It's true that organizers work weird hours and are always on call. Maybe it's for the best that they voted to keep a little pay differential in favor of the organizers.

Alex notices a police car on the next corner. Plastic bags scurry like rats down the dark street.

Bob Moses says that our understanding of how teaching works is often backward: the key to instruction is not for students to figure out what is in the teacher's head but for the teachers to figure out what is in the student's head. The vignette about "Alex" and the other scenarios that are scattered through part 1 are meant to give readers some idea of what is going on in the minds of the young people that I have worked with over the last twenty years. I am not trying to represent the students. They must do that for themselves. I am giving form, rather, to *how I understand* what the young people experience in the strange context of the Baltimore Algebra Project. Each of the vignettes derives from countless conversations with Baltimore City students. They are all centered on actual events that I have witnessed and that students have discussed with me. Some are composite, but all are "real" in the sense that many people would recognize their own observations or experiences.

The language, however, is mostly mine. It is how I talk to myself about how the young people talk to themselves. I do not have the novelist's gift of imagining myself to be someone other than who I am. But I do have some skill, I would say, at imagining myself to be in someone else's shoes. That is, I have listened to my students, watched them well enough, sat up with them at night, and marched with them enough to understand something about how they confront the world. Ultimately, the vignettes are guesses. But I decided to include these guesses rather than rely on transcripts of interviews (excepting the section "Kat and Alanis" in chapter 3), because I am making an argument that is not necessarily my students' argument. "They" are actually many, varied in outlook and belief, unpredictable in all the ways that human beings are, so I can't be sure they all share my viewpoint in all things; in fact, I know they don't.

Nevertheless, my argument is strengthened if readers have some sense of what I am responding to when I describe parallel educational institutions and youth enterprises. I am responding to what I think is in the students' heads and in their bodies and in their hearts.

Desegregation

This is a book about education and desegregation. But it is not primarily about desegregating races. It is about desegregating generations and age groupings. It is about desegregating the school "subjects." It is about desegregating education from politics and economics. It is about desegregating the past and the present and the future. It is about desegregating our peculiarly walled-up visions of who can do what.

"In the post–Civil Rights era," writes Theresa Perry, "the school is usually conceptualized singularly as an educational institution, failing to understand that for school to be a powerful institution for African Americans, it must also function as a cultural, social, and political institution."[1] The weight of history presses down like an enormous machine to separate schools from the rest of Black culture and often from the rest of Latinx, Indigenous, and Asian culture too. This enormous segregating die isolates students with one kind of test score from students with another, isolates teachers from the history of the community they teach in, and isolates the school system's finances from the economies of the families involved—the scraping for rent or bus money, the vulnerability of day labor and food stamps. Deracinated, rootless, the schools our children attend are too truncated to function as social, cultural, political, and economic institutions, and so they fail at education too.

There is an alternative. This book describes a way to integrate a system of education into the life of our people. It despises the segregating boundaries of schools, while acknowledging the current existence of those boundaries. It centers on what people, young and old, already know and do wherever they are, in school or out, but especially on what they do with "life as they find it, making it better."[2]

The Power in the Room[3]

We who believe in freedom are devising a system of education for a democracy that does not yet exist.[4] This is not about students achieving success by America's current standards: income, status, property, and patriarchal authority. The young people we describe will likely succeed in some way and will help each other and many of the rest of us live better lives. But we are not concerned with "making schools work," an odd and ahistorical task; we are thinking about the flowering of cultures, a frequent occurrence during thousands of years of human existence. The key characteristic of the students we work with will be that they stop deferring to the powerful and that they collectively take on the work of making better arrangements for their lives than other people have done for them so far.

We call this an "earned insurgency": "insurgency" because the powerful rely on an attitude of deference to keep the less powerful in their places; and "earned" because an insurgency will only succeed if it is built on a deep understanding of the significance of the struggle for justice, an understanding that must be arrived at through a process of disciplined and sustained effort, both individual and collective. What conditions are necessary to create that understanding and effort is the question we address.

As in a guerrilla war, the early stages of such an earned insurgency are partly camouflaged or disguised—often right out in the open but blending into the surrounding landscape so that the enemy will misinterpret it, see it for other than what it is. The exchanges of knowledge between young people "peer-to-peer" that are described and elaborated below are camouflage, but at the same time these exchanges function in other ways than merely to hide and cover. The social forms that this book promotes are innocuous and commonplace from a certain point of view. In our core example (only one example among many), students learn mathematics from each other in a laudable and entirely conventional activity. But the young people learning math consciously and deliberately from and with each other—carving out an autonomous space for themselves under a system of oppression—are not learning the same thing that students are learning from a well-paid teacher in a school of privilege.

Our guerrilla students are not simply learning how to solve quadratic equations or to recognize patterns in the slopes of tangents to a parabola. Learning is always contextual, interpersonal, reflective, and creative. Doing math looks like the typical occupation of the typical American adolescent, but while they do math, the young people are also learning how to resist the debilitating lessons of oppression and how to create and possess their own culture, their own representations and representative acts, their own world.

There is a public school in Baltimore that the system claims is "alternative," although its practices are very much like the practices of the other mainstream public schools. Students here are said to be "over-age and under-credited," which means that they are sixteen or seventeen or eighteen years old and still absurdly assigned to the sixth or seventh grade. The students have been placed here because the school system's administrators don't want them contaminating the other segregated buildings in their control. The system has some plan to accelerate them through the high school academic disciplines so they can earn credits with miraculous rapidity and graduate in another year or two. But they have no math teacher. The public school system finds it difficult to recruit enough math teachers. One was supposed to arrive from the Philippines before the start of the school year, but there was trouble with a visa, so the class is being managed by a long-term substitute who knows very little math. This is not an unusual problem in the United States. In 2015–16, forty-two states reported a shortage of math teachers, unevenly distributed, of course, between wealthier and less wealthy jurisdictions.[5]

This school represents an embarrassing failure of our current arrangements. The students are shunted here because they don't comply even enough to be passed on from grade to grade, and so they have become too old to sit in an age-segregated middle school classroom. Now it happens that certain high-level officials in the central administration have recently recognized that over-aged and under-credited students have trouble communicating with their teachers. So these officials have arranged to get some help from the youth-run, peer-to-peer economic enterprise known as the Baltimore Algebra Project. Most of the workers in this organization are high school students. None are older than twenty-four, as stipulated in the organization's bylaws. They are almost all African-ancestored, and many attend or recently attended the same schools that the under-credited students flunked out of.

The Algebra Project Math Literacy Workers are truly extraordinary: confident, kind, funny, hard-working, understanding, demanding of their peers. They learned how to apply these characteristics to the bizarre and neglected setting of the alternative school by connecting themselves to the rich history of the Black freedom struggle and by working in a youth-run enterprise that demanded certain virtues of them, certain strategies for coping with adversity. They have also learned to do math, that is, to make it their own, to represent themselves and their experiences in the language of mathematics. Not all of them are expert or even unusually knowledgeable. But they do math, they can do math, and they want to do math.[6] They get paid—they would not be able to work in the alternative school if they were not paid (they would need to find income elsewhere). But they are also passionate and committed to the education of their peers.

Parents, students, communities, scholars, activists need to ask: How can we recognize the young people in the room—the under-credited and the math literacy workers together—as already sufficient to create whatever education they need even without an imported teacher from the Philippines, from a suburb, from another state, from outside the community? Some adults who know math may figure in our answer, but they aren't in the room right now. What would we have to understand so that we can see the young people already in the room as capable of finding what they need, or of demanding what they need—from themselves, from their peers, and from the larger world around them? How do we have to change our vision to see them that way, and what needs to be in place for our vision to change? These are the questions we are trying to explain and answer.

The question is still the same if we picture a math classroom in a school of poverty with a fully certified math teacher but one in which the students don't do math anyway, don't want to do math, and believe they can't do math. What would we have to understand so that we could recognize the young people in *that* classroom also as already sufficient to create whatever education they need? How do we go from "They don't want to learn; they don't care; their parents don't care; they are too traumatized; a few might be saved, but most are hopeless cases" to a picture of insurgent agency—in the very same room with the very same students? The purpose of this book is to describe an education system that does not yet exist except in fragments but is a real education, not the delirium-inducing masquerade that we have tolerated too long. Not a system of education that reproduces racialized caste again and again but a system that ends that nightmare, at least in some extended pieces of geography, starting with those that the country traditionally has insisted it doesn't need, like ghettos, or housing projects, or rural backwaters, or Indigenous lands.

Though ambitious, this project of building a different relationship between young people and their own education is also straightforward and even simple in essence. It rests on a basic and easily observable fact: we human beings are actually good at organizing ourselves to achieve our purposes. All around us every day are the most amazing structures—physical, cultural, psychological, even political—that let many of us do the work we set out for ourselves and that let almost all of us achieve at least some of what we intend to do. This remarkable human world in which we exist has emerged from people just like us. The essential premise of democracy—not a fact like the structures around us but an indispensable premise if we are actually committed to the idea of equality—is that no group of people is particularly special—not the rich, not the Europeans, not men, not the people at the founding, not straight people but not gay people either, not the poor, not the oppressed—we are all just more or less the same in our natural capacities. If human beings have been able to create the structures we see around us, we can also create structures to suit our purposes and educate ourselves for democracy. Examples abound, many right within existing institutions that have developed out of the African American and other struggles. The great encourager, Vincent Harding, taught us that we will only need two things to build a new world: more creativity than we have ever exercised before (that seems like a relatively simple challenge) and more generosity than we have ever allowed (that seems a little harder).[7]

Crawl Spaces

We begin in a crawl space but look for ways to emerge into the open. The peer-to-peer youth enterprise structure will keep us camouflaged for a while. A crawl space is a physical and symbolic location occupied by people pushed down by the dominant society, but it's also a place where it has nevertheless become possible both to stay hidden in some way and also to try out new possibilities in relationship, representation, work, feeling, or expression. For the Algebra Project, math classes in schools of poverty are crawl spaces in this sense. They are "hidden" because the dominant society does not expect anything to come of them and so tends to leave them alone. But they can be fertile ground for trying out new ways of teaching and new social relations. The authorities do try to flatten crawl spaces if they become aware of them. But the math classroom is an interesting phenomenon, because sometimes the authorities' own rhetoric inadvertently opens up some room for freedom and experimentation. In this case, the representatives of oppression can't stop talking about the importance of STEM and how they would like all students to love math and be technologically or scientifically well-informed citizens and workers.

They don't mean what they say. If they did, then math classes in schools for poor children would have twelve or fifteen students per class, not thirty, and the teachers who are most skilled and experienced would teach the children who needed the most skilled teaching. But the authorities' protestations open up a crawl space: if we demonstrate that we are working on math, they may let us keep doing what we're doing. Democracies try to avoid the dirty work of state violence by perpetuating scams to keep people in their places "peacefully." Democracies don't like to have the curtain thrown back and the fraud revealed. This is the insight of the 1960s, when the hypocrisy of Southern Whites was exposed. They had contended—after lynching their way to purportedly quiescent

Black masses—that the sharecroppers and domestic workers were happy living under White rule. But when thousands of Black citizens started lining up to register to vote, White misrepresentations of Black acquiescence were exposed, and the power structure shook a little. There is a similar opening today around mathematics and other symbolic languages of science and technology. The authorities insist that everyone must be scientifically and mathematically literate, but they refuse to make the necessary arrangements to ensure that mathematical literacy is available to students in poverty. So the students must organize themselves in their crawl spaces till they are ready to stand up and demand access.[8]

We have an initial sense of what this looks like in practice. Students in the Baltimore Algebra Project have won a limited right to teach some of their peers math for a wage. The city and the school system pay the students for this work. They pay the students despite the fact that the Baltimore Algebra Project is notorious for calling out officials, disrupting meetings, and protesting. The city and school system still pay for the students' peer-to-peer math teaching, because doing math is a crawl space created by the unique circumstances of the twenty-first-century economy.

The action these students have taken to call the bluff of Baltimore officials is what we mean by earned insurgency. The students master some material and teach it to each other; they learn a little about how to speak forcefully in public; how to organize meetings, classes, conferences, demonstrations, research projects, and training workshops. Confronted by determined, accomplished, and persistent young people, the authorities find themselves conceding some ground. And the young people are consistent in demanding wages for their work. These and other students can emerge from crawl spaces into increasingly viable youth enterprises.

A Way Out

There are literally thousands of teachers and other adults in poor communities all over the country who are doing fascinating work with young people, both inside and outside mainstream schools.

They have discovered many kinds of crawl spaces: local history or environmental projects, construction or maker projects, research into race or gender inequities, media production and critique, farming, athletics, dance, drama, and music. Young people are attracted because the projects are fun or engaging, because they like the adults or older youth involved, or because they feel useful and somehow free. There is always, inevitably, a degree of political consciousness and analysis in these projects. It's a small step, then, to say, "We've learned something doing this work, and we want to share what we know with our peers. We should be paid to involve others, because knowledge is a valuable commodity in the twenty-first century, and we need the wages to survive and to continue our education."

The key is structuring young people's academic development at least partially through youth-operated economic enterprises that work parallel to school systems, not necessarily as part of them. Two such enterprises in Baltimore, for example, the Algebra Project and Leaders of a Beautiful Struggle, have involved thousands of young people over more than a decade in peer-to-peer knowledge work. The Algebra Project is grounded in math. Leaders of a Beautiful Struggle originated in competitive high school and college policy debate and has grown into a youth-centered think tank that uses research, organizing, and debate training to confront anti-Blackness and to promote Black institution-building. In these and a dozen other organizations in Baltimore, young people of high school age and recent graduates, overwhelmingly African-ancestored and working class, are paid—as members of collectives—to teach each other what they know. These youth-centered enterprises have a number of common characteristics that are described briefly here and elaborated in later sections.

1. They do knowledge work. Young people use their minds as well as their bodies to share knowledge and skills with peers and with their communities. This can involve any part of the human experience—art, athletics, math, science, history, journalism, video production, farming, environmental justice, carpentry, coding, and more.

2. The knowledge work is practical, creating tangible effects in the students' lives, for example, putting on a play, publishing a book or a video, rehabbing a house, running a sports league (coaching, refereeing, scheduling), or repairing computers or washing machines.

3. All students earn a significant wage in at least one youth-operated enterprise. In every working-class community today, young people need additional cash to help their families make ends meet. Other countries such as Germany and Holland offer cash allowances, paid uniformly for every child in the country but supported by progressive taxation so that wealthier families end up paying for their own and portions of other families' child allowances. Many voters in the United States find such an idea hard to accept politically, but they do not object as much to paying wages to adolescents. There can be several wage rates in each youth-operated enterprise, depending on the particular skill or the student's experience and level of responsibility in the enterprise. The young people can decide these rates collectively. No students should have to sell drugs, prostitute themselves, or work late hours in fast food restaurants at suburban malls just so they can pay their phone bills.

4. The work is indigenous. Student workers and leaders are native to the community whose youth participate in the enterprises. Any older facilitators, mentors, or teachers are also indigenous or are invited into the community by the young people and their families, as opposed to being assigned from external philanthropies, nonprofits, or government agencies.

5. Use of funds is controlled by the youth-operated enterprise, ideally as a local network of enterprises that share similar accounting, reporting, financial control, and governance procedures to support transparency and minimize malfeasance. This financial work is itself highly educative and important.

6. Decision processes are authentically participatory. Members of these youth-operated enterprises do more than simply vote. The organizational structures are designed to warn against and counteract concentrations of power in the hands of a few. The models for this work are the Young Negroes' Cooperative League of the 1930s and the Student Nonviolent Coordinating Committee of the 1960s. Both were instructed in their organizing and economic strategies by Ella Baker, "a black feminist even before the term was invented [who] . . . criticized unchecked egos, objected to undemocratic structures, protested unilateral decision making, condemned elitism, and refused to nod in loyal deference to everything 'the leader' had to say."[9]

7. Roles are built-in for successive generations as the work continues. Students who graduate from high school after working with one of the youth-operated enterprises sometimes choose to stay involved in teaching or facilitating roles. They function as mentors, instructors, troubleshooters, mediators, fund-raisers, generally tasked with ensuring the success of the younger members of the collective but careful not to usurp the democratic power of their mentees. Elders in the community steeped in the ethos of indigenous self-determination also find mutually nourishing work with the younger people who are at the center. The elders' role is to preserve historical knowledge and wisdom, while accepting that it will be adapted by young people to new circumstances. None of this needs to be done for free. Recognition is given to the material needs of all generational layers in the community.

Mira, the business manager, has to get home, because Bryan is watching the girls, and if she doesn't get there soon, he will be late for work. But she can't leave yet—the accounts aren't reconciling right. She feels sleepy after the meal her boyfriend, Sherrod, brought her from McDonald's on his way to the tutoring site. It's hard to concentrate. People are texting, asking if the checks will be ready tomorrow, but she has to do the reconcile report before she can call in payroll, and the reconcile keeps messing up. She can't find the mistake: $500 and some change that the bank says went out of the account. Someone forgot to process a payment correctly, or stole it.

Mira is eighteen, just starting college. Two little girls at home, Salima and Crystal, a two-year-old and a six-month-old baby. She should have brought them to work with her. She'll have to stay up late anyway to finish her paper for English. And the rent is due. She and Sherrod need those checks tomorrow too. Sherrod gets $240 every two weeks for tutoring after school. She brings home almost $400 as the business manager.

Bryan, Sherrod's little brother, lives with them and sleeps on the sofa at their apartment. He doesn't help with the rent, but he also doesn't charge to babysit, and he's very good with the girls when their grandmother can't watch them. It would be better if he kept some kind of regular hours, and he should have been in school today anyway, but he only goes when he feels like it. Convenient today, because otherwise Mira would have had to bring the girls to work. Bryan really needs to go to school, but he says it's a waste of time. He prefers to be useful watching his nieces and working with Sherrod at the tutoring site.

Building Parallel Institutions

Many practitioners of liberation politics have understood their work to involve the creation of parallel institutions. In Baltimore, youth-operated enterprises effectively create a parallel educational structure. Young people learn to read, write, speak, quantify, and analyze data through their authentic need to communicate as they operate their enterprises assisting peers and others in their neighborhoods. They also learn all kinds of specific technical skills based on the range of enterprises that a community generates. In all of them, young people share knowledge and skills with peers, earn a wage, and participate collectively in governance. Since 2002 the students in Baltimore have earned more than $4 million in wages through this kind of employment. Several organizations are currently working on coordinating such enterprises into a stronger network so that they can collectively represent themselves as fulfilling formal educational functions of the community, at least in part.

No one is admitted to or excluded from any of these enterprises because of adult evaluations of any kind. In fact, students from both the highly selective high schools and the nonselective schools collaborate without status distinctions. Students with identified special needs are included by their peer groups on the model of a family (or, more technically, as a "base community," described in chapter 5)[10] rather than by institutional formulas and divisions. One youth enterprise, supported by the Disability Rights Maryland law center, has taken it upon themselves to coach others (as well as coaching adults) in how to attend consistently to the needs of specific young people in the context of the general work. They get paid for this consultancy and are able to bring a student's-eye view to the problem, bonding with their peer collaborators in the process.[11]

Similarly, youth-operated enterprises pay attention to how their members will get home at night, where they will sleep if they are homeless, how their younger siblings or their own children will be cared for (at the worksite if necessary), and how they will eat. Rather than seeing different parts of the community as segregated—people who can afford transportation versus people who can't; people with childcare responsibilities versus people without—we try to build a network of organizations that integrate needs, families, and resources, holding people together. These practices are merely an extension and formalization of the mutual aid ethos that has always sustained oppressed people.

Schools recognize that "social determinants" play a significant role in students' lives, but they can't think much beyond coordinating "services" that come from outside the school. Most schools of poverty are not in fact organized to support whole, functionally integrated cultures. They are organized very effectively to measure and set in relief the difference between the dominant culture and the students' culture. *Outside* of schools, however, in our community-based enterprises, the logic of measurement is subordinated to the logic of meeting real needs. It would make no sense to operate a tutoring site as a place of learning, employment, and cultural solidarity if young people couldn't attend because of transportation or childcare or hunger. So the young people address these needs as primary, always remembering that the wages play a crucial role in buying some flexibility about how arrangements will be made.

A Figured Universe

Youth-determined educational and economic structures are also important for cognitive reasons. The more integrated and workable the different parts of a student's life, the more the student looks to find patterns, causal relations, and regularities that will help with solving problems. When a child's life is filled with disconnected parts, the skills necessary to survive are built around coping with expected arbitrariness, not expected patterns. One way to describe institutional racism is to say that the proportion of arbitrary institutional effects on people of color is higher than the proportion of arbitrary institutional effects on White people. Broadly, dominant institutions make sense for White people, and they don't make sense for people of color. The so-called achievement gap is just a measure of the difference between how much sense our educational institutions make to different races and classes. In institutions that generally meet their needs, children use predictable patterns to advance their own interests. In institutions filled with arbitrary pain and humiliation, with violence and threats of violence, children don't waste their time looking for predictable patterns; they maintain a low profile and reserve their analytical skills for places where they experience more control, or they act out freely in rebellion. Furthermore, when well-funded and attention-grabbing services mostly originate from outside the immediate community rather than being indigenous, creativity that might have been used to find local solutions is shifted toward creativity in gaining access to external patronage of various kinds, almost always resulting in one form or another of exploitation or incapacity.

In contrast, Baltimore's youth-operated enterprises enact an often racially segregated but socially integrated "figured universe" so beautifully described by Theresa Perry in "Up from the Parched Earth: Toward A Theory of African-American Achievement." Perry describes the creation of "as-if" worlds in which relationships based on justice and mutuality ground intellectual effort and commitment.[12] In protected space where experienced actors model intellectual and cultural collaboration, children develop identities as learners planning for futures in relationship to each other and to their communities. Rather than deferring to the larger society's monetized abstractions and sortings, young people are encouraged and taught how to meet their material and cultural needs through assertions of their own, writing their own historically informed script: "Here's how we should get our work done so that we accomplish our concrete purposes. We don't need to feel immobilized by someone else's coercive, violence-saturated structures."

With this grounding, young people have constructed a base of power that is partially insulated from the institutional dynamics of schools. They do not need to seek approval from school authorities to undertake community-based projects or mobilizations. They do not need to comply with hierarchical standards on what constitutes learning. Where they are, what they do, and when they do it is not determined by a school schedule but is agreed on by their peer group and geographically situated community, based on the needs of the work they have decided to pursue. In other words, they move their bodies in self-determined freedom.

What underlies this approach is the understanding that the parts of a life cannot be fragmented and disconnected if we want children to grow up with a sense of wholeness and integrity. Students who feel whole cannot be judged by their teachers for the language that their parents speak or feel that their dialect is somehow not fit for learning because it is always corrected in school. They cannot feel that their material needs must always be postponed, disconnecting the present and the future. They cannot constantly fear that certain expressions of gender or sexuality will be despised or excluded. They cannot see a world on television that has an idealized, integrated middle-class culture and look down their actual street to see only trash and dilapidated housing inhabited by an apparently quarantined, caged race. These fragments and dissociations of time and space will not lead young people from an eager, impressionable childhood into an adulthood of confident exploration and inquiry.

But the youth-operated enterprises that are burgeoning here in Baltimore and elsewhere create viable mini-societies that young people experience as, to some extent, complete. These mini-societies have something of the same completeness as a well-organized gang. You get a little money. You feel useful, performing a role that helps the group. You see an attractive future within reach, because the members of your organization who are only a year or two older than you already know a little more, have more responsibility, earn a bit more money, and look out for you, or chastise you when you mess up. The college-age adult mentors and leaders are elevated even further. You may have a greater awareness of what's going on around you than others on your block, being on the inside of something powerful, lucrative, and stylish, instead of just on the outside of the society you watch in movies and on TV; but this inside is open to any of your peers who ask to enter. People make sure you don't go hungry and that you have a place to sleep when things get really bad. And there is lots of fun, adventure, challenge, humor, and, of course, romance. Your parents are proud of the money you bring home from doing something positive; you may even ease some tensions in the family by contributing economically and by accepting a more adult role.

What you learn doing knowledge work in a youth-operated enterprise is therefore connected and integrated with other parts of your life. And feeling whole, rather than fragmented, you become able, over time, to enter the larger world beyond your neighborhood with a sense of integrity and authority derived from the high-functioning mini-society that you and your peers sustain.

The parallel educational structure I've described is rooted in the needs of young people, not in a caste ordering that directs material and social goods according to today's patterns. Because the caste ordering is not its goal, this parallel structure can do without sorting students into various putative "ability" groups. And because it can do without that kind of sorting, there is no use for violence and threats of violence to compel attendance of specific bodies in specific places.

This does not mean that there are no rules, no need for young people to show up to work at a certain time, or no structure. But the principle that requires their attendance and conformity to group norms is not a principle of merit or qualification established by state authority on the "evidence" of grades, test scores, and behavioral records. The principle that requires their attendance and participation is, rather, a formalization of peer and community relationships that has evolved in each particular group to get the work accomplished that the group has agreed to do.

Nor is the effectiveness of such a structure far-fetched. In 2018 alone, government and nonprofit agencies in Baltimore contracted with half a dozen of these youth-operated entities for hundreds of thousands of dollars' worth of work—work that made sense to the young people involved. They didn't show up to do this work because of a grade they would receive. They showed up because of a contract. But wages alone do not guarantee high quality performance, initiative, or responsible behavior. These qualities—often, though not always on display—result from individual and collective understanding of the importance of the tasks undertaken. They are qualities of the culture that the young people—protected and supported by knowledgeable and caring adults—have created for themselves. Though the culture varies somewhat from group to group, it shares many features, including historical and social analysis, ways of mediating conflict, and norms of collective and individual self-criticism. The youth culture derives from the work of generations that came before as urged and taught by elders and mentors, but it is also adapted by the youngest for their own purposes.

As in any classroom, program, African-centered or community-organized school where young people come to understand their own power, what is obvious in youth-operated enterprises is that students have a changed relationship to learning. These embryonic institutions are places where it feels natural and therefore easy for knowledge to be produced and exchanged. The learning that takes place in these enterprises may or may not match, formality by formality, the materials printed in textbooks. But the formal structures of knowledge used by the young people serve concrete purposes in their classroom or community. Just as in spaces described, for example, by Bettina Love, Christopher Emdin, Rochelle Gutiérrez, Leigh Patel, and many other outstanding teachers and researchers, the young people involved in peer-to-peer enterprises use experience to construct schema that work for them in their interactions with the world around them, starting from their own culture's ways of confronting oppression.[13] Peer-to-peer youth enterprises define young people's economic need as a crucial element of this struggle.

When high school students in a community arts center are paid to research indigenous local histories in preparation for painting a mural and they take four or five middle schoolers under their wing in the process, they are learning and teaching in a culturally relevant way, partly because earning money is culturally relevant. When students are paid to develop training videos on how youth experience encounters with police and when they then involve peers and police in dialogue around the videos, they are learning and teaching in a culturally relevant way. And when the young people involved in work like this begin to understand themselves as earners, as people who can monitor income and expenses, who can investigate the way money is earned and spent, who are eligible to decide how resources might be allocated—for example, more to them, less to the police—they are able to reflect and to act on their world in new ways, leading to new learning.

There is no telling where this adventure will end. The Algebra Project and organizations like it support young people who refuse the sorting and violence of school in favor of a parallel materially and culturally viable network. Whether networks such as these actually work is not in doubt. There are many historical instances of figured universes and many examples across the country and across the world, besides the network in Baltimore, in which oppressed communities step outside the dominant educational structures and create wholesome ways for young people to grow to adulthood—in families, churches, Black independent schools, community organizations, and elsewhere.

The only open question is whether parallel institutions like these can be grown and sustained using some kind of pragmatic structure like that of the youth-operated enterprises described here. What is at stake is self-determination, as opposed to other-determination. For people in poverty, other people's power constrains possibility. To determine our own futures will require arrangements that replace the existing arrangements, because what exists now does not serve our needs. The future cultural forms arrived at by a self-determining people are unknowable, though we know they will be different from the forms twisted into tortured coexistence with an oppressive system.

CHAPTER 2

Solving Our Own Problems

CMG liked nothing better than playing basketball, but he never missed the annual football game the day after Christmas in the park on the other side of the road from his mother's house. Twenty of his friends and his little brother. Tackle, no pads. No one could catch him when he was in his flow. Spinning and feinting, elated.

It was good to have a little break from work. People expected a lot of him. He spoke at rallies. The new mayor knew his name. The old mayor—now the governor—hated him for starting a campaign to block his pet project of constructing a new youth jail. Although CMG was usually the one interviewed on TV, no one thought he was stuck up, because what he liked best was basketball at the playground or *Call of Duty* in his living room with all the people he had known since second grade coming in and out of his mother's rowhouse as if it was their own home. His mother worked late most days, but when she was home, she always cooked, and never minded how many friends were over. She felt best when the house was full of those rowdy, respectful boys. They kept each other safe.

In seventh grade he used to go to the high school most afternoons for help with his math. In ninth grade he became an Algebra Project tutor himself. Then he started bringing all his friends to demonstrations and rallies, and the older organizers noticed how he always traveled with a crew. When he was elected lead organizer in eleventh grade, things really started to open up. His committee went to conferences and events all over the country talking and organizing around youth power, and once he found himself speaking on the same stage as Angela Davis. Her topic was prison abolition. His topic was youth jobs and the Algebra Project slogan: "No Education, No Life!"

CMG found his composition book and started to write about the football game he would play on the first day of Kwanzaa, about Black love, and about where he would find money to go back to college when the winter break ended. Maybe he wouldn't go back. He already owed thousands of dollars. The rhymes about oppression and freedom flowed like his dancing feet on the court, on the field, on the stage of the world.

Some Examples

We know enough to recognize that deference to the current educational structures based on "merit" and "qualification" should end; those structures are just as calamitous as police violence. Because young people feel the threat and the actual violence of the education system in their bodies, we older people must validate, not undermine, their conviction that many schools do them physical and psychological harm. This validation can be achieved by supporting new educational structures in which young bodies and minds can grow up intact and connected to one another and to the world. Sorting necessitates violence, but education is freedom, and the realization of a true democracy will require new forms of education, including new economic and political relationships that young people are already qualified to enact and refine.

Exchanging knowledge peer-to-peer as a form of collective employment creates opportunities in a new political economy parallel to the one that currently exists in the education world. Rather than seeing schools and school systems as the only economic and organizational engines in the distribution of knowledge, we can recognize the growth and development of another economic and organizational engine that builds on community-based efforts to put young people to work distributing and generating knowledge for and with their peers and neighbors. There are two important characteristics to note: First, the parallel political economy rewards boldness in the participants. They do not need to defer to someone else's definition of culture. This is, of course, a stance that many young people naturally occupy with delight. But beyond simply enacting youthful rebellion, the peer-to-peer economic institutions that we are developing show in pragmatic ways how young people can arrange their lives to meet their actual needs without deferring to the dominant paradigms.

Second, the parallel political economy does not need to be entirely walled off from the dominant political economy of schooling. Almost all the young people involved in our network or ecosystem also go to school or college. We might simply picture this as actors performing in two theaters on different days—say a big, established theater, and a smaller upstart. The actors play different roles on the different stages; the norms and cultures of the troupes might be quite different, but the performers somehow cope with going back and forth. The one may even be contained in the other as a kind of rehearsal space where a teacher has figured out how to develop a semi-autonomous site of student agency within an existing school, or where a brave charter or independent school has chipped out an area of self-determination. One theater is much healthier, more satisfying, more vibrant and instructive for its actors. Eventually it will attract audiences and resources in competition with the other, more established theater, but initially it is too small and apparently insignificant to be much of a threat.

The parallel educational culture that we in Baltimore are developing through our network of peer-to-peer youth enterprises is growing on its own, but it is also developing in relation to the existing structure of public and private education. The relationship is complicated and multifaceted; I discuss some of the complications below. But we do not need to have a definite picture of where the systems will end up in relation to each other. For now, we just need to establish the viability of our parallel political economy, its relative autonomy, its ability to satisfy many of the young people's needs, and its vibrant connection to their historical cultures.

Many examples of paid peer-to-peer knowledge exchange currently exist. The descriptions below, mostly of programs in Baltimore, give a sense of both the potential scope and also the relative simplicity of each enterprise, even when the shared knowledge is quite technical. To the extent possible, these enterprises are structured by the young people involved—both wage earners and the peers who are receiving instruction. Youth in the twenty- to thirty-year-old age range with experience in peer-to-peer work have full-time employment in roles that support these enterprises. Readers will certainly know many more such programs and projects in their own areas—maybe not yet paying a wage but where young people are doing work that easily could be compensated if funds were available. The wonderful work they do, of course, distracts many policymakers from the insurgent space these enterprises create for building norms of solidarity, autonomy, and radical purpose.

In each case, I am describing structures in which a few young people of color or young people in poverty, roughly ages fourteen to twenty-five, (1) have mastered some chunk of knowledge—either on their own or taught by someone older or by a peer, and (2) are receiving a wage to share or use what they know to benefit their peers and community.

- *Policy debate:* The members of Leaders of a Beautiful Struggle, which was formed by young men and women now in their twenties and early thirties, have mastered the methods of policy debate and are employed coaching high school and middle school debate teams as well as running a summer camp for high school debaters. They also earn revenue through extensive antiracist workshops, policy convenings, and publication, and they are significant players in Baltimore's political scene.

- *Media production:* Many groups, such as Afrikan Youth Alchemy, New Lens, and Wide Angle Media, employ young people who have mastered videography, editing, writing, and marketing skills to teach their peers how to create videos on many different issues, including health, police violence, and youth employment. They contract with city agencies and nonprofits, which use the videos for instructing and informing employees or the public.

- *Math and organizing:* Young people of the Baltimore Algebra Project run after-school math programs and a math/basketball summer camp. High school and college students also coteach in regular school math classes. This paid math work forms an organizing base for student self-advocacy and political organizing.

- *Environmental policy and practice:* United Workers establishes teams of organizers to mobilize around environmental issues in oppressed communities. United Workers also hires young people to run their own food-scrap collection enterprise, educating peers in composting.

- *Athletic leagues:* Camp Elevate hires young people to run a community-based basketball summer league with support from twenty- to thirty-year-olds. Youth are paid to coach and manage teams, to referee games, and to maintain schedules, standings, awards ceremonies, and venue bookings.

- *Health education teams:* Young people trained by Planned Parenthood, traveling in small groups, go to where other young people are (schools, playgrounds, transportation hubs, malls, corners) and engage peers in public health outreach and education through activities they develop (games, spoken word) on topics including sexual and reproductive health, nutrition, first aid and CPR, addiction, and antiviolence work.

- *Agricultural enterprises:* Working with adults and younger children, young people under the auspices of Pleasant Hope Baptist Church grow, market, and consume their own food while studying African American agrarian history.

- *Paralegal teams:* Teams of young people with basic knowledge of legal systems and procedures accompany peers as advocates to hearings or meetings with officials, write letters, advise on steps to cope with issues such as eviction, discrimination, run-ins with police, immigration rights, and access for peers with disabilities.

- *Oral history:* Youth and young adults train peers in creating media presentations based on oral history for community narrative projects either self-initiated or commissioned by, for example, neighborhood associations, university researchers, government agencies, and museums.

- *Theater:* WombWork Productions hires young people to teach peers how to produce community-based plays, working with original scripts or scripts from the published repertoire.

- *Poetry:* DewMore Baltimore employs young people to teach poetry writing, publication, and performance, contracting with dozens of schools around the city.

- *Music:* Victorious Productions hires young people to teach instrumental and vocal music to peers, operate recording studios, and produce public performances, at school or in the community.

- *Math, science, engineering, art, and technology centers and makerspaces:* The Young People's Project hires young people to teach number theory and coding both in school and after school. 901 Arts and Intersection of Change pay young people to share arts skills with peers. STEAM centers employ near-peers to teach technology and art skills.

- *Trades:* Young adults teach near-peers the basics of barbering at Conscious Heads; sewing and fabric work enterprises grow out of classes at Unique Fabrics Sewing Program for Women and Girls; carpentry, wiring, and plumbing are facilitated by near-peers actually performing work in community homes, supervised by licensed instructors.

- *Yoga and meditation:* The Holistic Life Foundation hires young people who lead peers in practicing physical, mental, and spiritual centering.

- *Reading groups:* Young people lead peers or younger near-peers in topic-oriented reading groups focused on, for example, sexuality, gender identity, ethnic studies, fantasy, or anime.

- *Language exchange:* A school-based club, Somos, employs mixed language teams (for example, native Spanish and native English speakers) to lead conversation groups for peers and adults on topics of interest to them, for the purpose of developing conversational fluency and overcoming cultural barriers. The members of the club write and print bilingual newspapers and distribute bilingual books and newspapers.

- *Accounting/bookkeeping:* Each peer-to-peer enterprise needs to keep account of its finances. Teams of peers teach others how to create budgets, use online accounting programs, process payroll, and produce cash-flow statements.

- *Research and evaluation:* Participatory sociological or environmental research teams develop research questions and methods, gather and analyze data, and publish results for the community or a wider audience.

- *Credit union:* Students operate a full-service credit union, creating savings and debit accounts, and establishing loan procedures tied to electronic monthly payments deducted directly from students' wages in their peer-to-peer enterprise.

- *Journalism:* Video, radio, or print news outlets made up of student reporters, techs, and graphic artists develop their own investigative or thematic projects for publication and distribution.

All of these examples of skill and knowledge exchanges are practical; in fact, these enterprises have already emerged between peers and near-peers, sometimes starting in informal contexts on a small scale. There is nothing particularly fancy about them or beyond the capabilities of young people in any community. What is missing is a consciousness of shared purpose among the exchanges, and a political and economic commitment to build them out. If they can be organized into a network of social enterprises, they will create a platform for young people to both reflect and act on their roles as producers of knowledge, or—in cultural rather than economic terms—as creators of culture.

Buying Time

The idea of monetizing young people's knowledge creates fascinating arguments. Many young people themselves say that they would be happy to share what they know for free, as volunteers, and they are certainly telling the truth. But they usually can't afford the time. If a money-making opportunity comes along that competes with voluntarily helping their peers, they must go where the money is.

Part of the education scam is indoctrinating young people into the view that earning money from knowledge requires a credential—a credential that can only be acquired at some distant time in the future. Lawyers can charge $300 an hour because they have earned so many degrees. High school students' knowledge can't be monetized yet, because they haven't worked their way through the system that verifies knowledge or skills as legitimate.

But this argument is nonsense. If you know something and can share what you know, it is likely someone will want to learn from you. The problem is that the peer "customers" of teenagers in poverty are poor themselves, and they can't afford to pay. The root of the problem does not lie in the *value* of the teenagers' knowledge. Rather, it lies in our willingness as a society to pay for something of undisputed value. No individual family can afford to buy a snow plow, not to mention a tank or a nuclear weapon. We organize capital in such a way that the community pays for those purchases collectively. The community could also organize capital in such a way that it can afford to pay teenagers for teaching what they know to their peers. Young people in poverty can be taught to demand decent wages for sharing what they know. The more ordinary this demand becomes, the easier it will be to organize around it and to make it a reality.

I am not talking about stipends. Many after-school programs staffed by middle-class adults providing "enrichment" for poor children pay stipends to their adolescent interns or "helpers"—$50 a month or a little more or a little less. The adolescent helpers and interns are, of course, thrilled. Compared to nothing, $50 a month for doing what you love is a lot. But stipends are not enough. I am describing youth enterprises—not adult enterprises with youth helpers. Adolescence is expensive for families. Teenagers take up more space than younger children. They need their own phones. They travel more, eat more, go out, care about their clothes. Poor families expect serious economic contributions from them. The young people need sufficient income that they can meet their needs and stay involved in an enterprise over many years if they want to, rising through the stages of their organization's knowledge structure as they mature and learn more, and pass on what they know to the next generations coming behind them.

Decent wages buy the students' time. Notice the contrast with the economics of middle-class families. Parents of wealthier students often advise their children *not* to work: "Your job is doing well in school." The parents' income is high enough to meet their own and their children's material needs and much more: not only allowances but also transportation, communication, clothing, food, entertainment, and fees for athletics, art, or music. For less wealthy families, it's hard to pay the rent, keep food on the table, do the laundry, get to work. Adolescents must contribute both to the family income and to their own upkeep, and they must find a way to participate in their peer group in and out of school—pay for trips, dates, prom—an endless cascade of costs.

A job handing out fast food at Burger King, often at a distant location and late into the night, can be debilitating. A job in knowledge work rooted in your own community is a different thing entirely. The wage buys your time; you can afford to be involved with your peers working on something that tangibly benefits you and your neighbors. And rather than being drained by your job, you learn concrete skills and also a worldview that puts you and your peers at the center of new possibilities for the present and the future.

Consciousness, Collectivism, and Cognition

Over fifteen years, young people in Baltimore have earned millions of dollars in enterprises that they largely control themselves. Because student workers' material needs begin to be met by wages, the students become available for growth in at least three areas, all three of which are already potentially active in any crawl space, even before an organization emerges as a full-fledged youth enterprise. Consciously promoting these areas of development helps build youth power. I introduce these areas here and look at them more closely later on.

First, because the youth enterprises emerge with some degree of political consciousness, the young people involved are not mere employees exchanging alienated labor for cash. They are members of organized collectives, and so they learn something about the economics of collectivism, exploring new property relations and new relations of production. A fourteen-year-old may find herself debating and voting on whether an older colleague should be allowed some extra money because he had an operation and is not able to work as many hours as he used to, or on how a contract with a school should be negotiated.

Second, members of youth-led organizations learn about the politics of collectivism. We live in a putatively democratic country where virtually all our institutions—schools, businesses, bureaucracies, most churches, the police and military—are presumed to be undemocratic. The closest we generally get to democracy in America is voting in elections. There are very few places where young people can experience themselves as central to the decision-making of an institution that affects their lives. The youth enterprises we are discussing offer exactly this experience: "No one *except* me and peers just like me can determine the direction of our collective." This is the fundamentally empowered creed of the peer-to-peer enterprises. All kinds of political lessons are learned in the process. How is authority earned? Who speaks well? Who backs up their arguments with evidence? Who follows through and does what they say they will do? Who is allied with whom? Whose analysis is superficial or short-sighted; whose is deeper and aimed at a powerful future? What do we do when we disagree? How do we keep our decision-making on course when we are hurt by or angry at a colleague or ally? These are crucial political questions that must come up as the collective tries to find its way forward with no one to give answers except its members.

The third area of potential growth in peer-to-peer organizations is cognitive development. There is now a large body of research on "communities of practice."[1] This research documents comprehensively how development as an apprentice among a group of already expert or at least advanced practitioners of some skill follows a regular process. Apprentices respond in relatively predictable patterns, moving through stages of awareness, ability, and incorporation into the ways of the group. The research, of course, documents what is already apparent in all societies: human beings learn the ways of their people. They imitate, they identify, they join up with people around them to accomplish both individual and collective purposes. In the process of this socialization, they learn things. Michael Halliday, a linguist, conjectures that all learning begins in the interpersonal mode. We learn, he argues, *because* we interact with each other.[2]

In contrast to today's schooling that treats the individual as primary, youth enterprises treat the collective as primary, because— among other reasons—such an emphasis is important for cognitive development. Youth-led organizations are classic examples of communities of practice, and as such they naturally provide a rich environment for cognitive development.

Four Problems: Literacy, Economics, Culture, and Legitimation

The challenge now is to build this peer-to-peer work out as a deliberate strategy for putting more control of education, economics, and politics directly in the hands of oppressed communities. In developing any peer-to-peer structure, we are looking for solutions to at least four problems:

1. *The problem of literacy:* How do young people become literate in the various systems of representation used today: verbal, mathematical, scientific, electronic, and visual, for example? This is the problem the mainstream education system typically addresses in its official policies.

2. *The problem of economics:* How can the material needs of students be satisfied in the current social context?

3. *The problem of culture:* How do young people come to represent themselves as a part of a collective with a past that establishes their dignity and a future that continues it?

4. *The problem of legitimation:* How can young people assure themselves and others that they are worth taking seriously, that they are using workable structures to build power?

Today's unhelpful dominant educational arrangements were developed over the past half century through conscious decisions by policymakers to "correct" four corresponding "deficits" in communities that are considered incapable of raising their own children:

1. Poor communities are populated by people who are mostly illiterate, so literate people from other communities must be imported to teach them.

2. Poor communities lack cash and capital, so transfer payments must flow from outside the jurisdiction in.

3. Poor communities have either an absence of culture or dysfunctional cultures, so cultural richness must be given to poor communities from outside.

4. People in poor communities are mostly without credentials and thus their legitimacy as teachers and role models is suspect, so people from outside must come in to certify them, when they are deserving.

The current educational arrangements in poor communities emerge concretely from this analysis of deficits, and from the "obvious" outside-in solutions to these deficits. For example: Teach for America (TFA) and other alternative certification programs are designed to address a shortage of qualified teachers by importing teachers from elsewhere. Notice that this "solution" addresses several of the deficits simultaneously: TFA teachers are presumed literate, of course, but they also are mostly from middle- and upper-middle-class families, so the under-resourced school system does not need to buy them personal laptops, for example, and their parents subsidize, say, their car insurance or moving expenses. Also, their credit is good, and they can borrow to cover current expenses, freeing up time to devote to lesson planning or research, while a teacher emerging out of a working-class family is more likely to need to take a second job while participating in TFA. Furthermore, TFA teachers bring considerable exogenous cultural and social capital with them into impoverished communities, hooking students up with rich opportunities and "exposure" to ideas, places, and experiences that the dominant culture insists are not easily accessible otherwise—but implicitly devaluing indigenous cultures in the process.

Curriculum "innovations" such as Common Core are another example. They address perceived cultural deficits by establishing in "plain" language the current dominant picture of proficiency. The various testing regimens developed around Common Core reflect not only what knowledge is central (from the dominant perspective, of course) but also the means by which we will certify that someone has acquired that knowledge. In both cases, outsiders assume that poor communities cannot recognize what knowledge is important or legitimate the acquisition of that knowledge for themselves.

Similarly, the shedding of arts, music, theater, and recreation from school curricula is perversely justified as for the students' own good. Policymakers theorize that poor students will need to impress corporate employers from outside the community if they ever want to get and keep a job; those corporate employers are looking for test results and "basic" skills, not creativity—at least not from the lowest tier of employees. Time and money must be focused on what produces the biggest skill-related bang for the education buck.

The financial deficits of inner-city school systems, as a final example, are tightly controlled by state governments through complicated legal structures, because the states are rich, while the cities are poor (often a direct consequence of White flight). Decisions about education funding are made outside poor communities: generally local school boards are unrepresentative of the families served by public schools, and even where they are elected, they have little real power, because power remains in the hands of those whose money is being transferred into the urban districts—mostly corporate, commercial, and suburban interests in every single state. Needless to say, these interests ensure that the bulk of the funds spent come back to the sectors where they originated.

I once enjoyed the spectacle of a Baltimore City School Board procurement meeting, during which various school system contracts were being formally awarded. Each contract was brought before the board, one at a time. The chair called for a vote. For each vote, two, three, or four of the nine board members would recuse themselves due to some conflict of interest—they served on the board of the vendor, or they worked for or owned shares in or had a personal connection with the firms that would earn revenue through the contract. The other five, six, or seven board members would unanimously approve the contract. The next item would be called up. Same rigmarole: two, three, or four recusals—but different members this time. Unanimous approval by the remaining members. And on and on through each contract for the evening. You scratch my back, I'll scratch yours. This is, of course, a microcosm of the

American system: great probity from public officials as demonstrated by their honorable rejection of obvious graft, in full confidence that as long as the system is working smoothly, they will
be rewarded, eventually, for their acquiescence in allowing *others*
to make lucrative deals, just not quite as immediately as in those
"undeveloped," less legally sophisticated countries where bribes are
quicker and more direct. Individually, each member is honest and
avoids even the appearance of self-dealing; collectively, the board
looks out for itself, accumulating more and more at the centers of
capitalist power. If the school board had been required to vote on
all the contracts at once, no business could have transpired, since all
the members would have been recused simultaneously through one
conflict of interest or another. But business must go on.

The strategy of developing peer-to-peer youth enterprises can
be understood at least in part as a scheme for liberating some funds
from that loop of accumulation so the money can circulate within
the communities that are supposed to benefit from public education
dollars rather than within powerful constituencies that are already
hooked up.

Four Already-Existing Strengths

As I have highlighted, various policies and practices of schooling in
poor communities derive from a belief that those communities are
in deficit and that solutions must come from outside. Our parallel
network, in contrast, is indigenous (grown from inside) and autochthonous (sprung from the land). We see our communities teeming
with rich cultures and filled with people literate in a whole variety of
representational systems. And we think of the twenty-first-century
economy not in terms of one or two segregated budgets—the school
system's budget, for example, or the state's, or this urban family's
budget or that suburban one—but as a huge multilayered flow of
both capital and liquidity that is more accurately described as con-
tiguous in geography and continuous in time than as discontinuous
and discrete. The boundaries of property are asserted for human
purposes; they are not natural boundaries. When we look at many of

Baltimore's decaying blocks where families still live, families whose children attend our schools, we should ask not only, "Whose property is this block now? Why does no one invest in it today?" but also "Whose property *was* this block? Whose money *was* invested in it? Whose labor built it? What was extracted from it? Where did the wealth go that it once represented? Where is that wealth now? What money still passes through it, concretely as cash, or abstractly as quantifiable symbolic assets?" Our communities are indeed starved for liquidity and capital, but they are only separated from wealthier places, and from wealth-generating times, by fictions, by boundaries human beings invented so that they could say, "This is mine, not yours." We will explore this concept of property and its relation to legitimacy in more detail below.[3]

In the meantime, what does an indigenous, autochthonous solution look like? Strengths that already exist can address the needs of poor communities while correcting dominant misconceptions. We already have all the resources needed to build a new economy of education.

1. People who can teach literacies of all kinds already live in poor communities, but they spend their time doing other things, because teaching literacies in poor communities—without the dominant culture's certification—usually doesn't feed their families or pay their bills.

2. There is more than enough liquidity and capital in the United States to meet everyone's material needs. This is the wealthiest country that has ever existed. Also, billions of dollars flow through each major city every year, ostensibly for the benefit of the poor. Very little of that cash stays or circulates in poor communities. Mostly the cash flows in and flows right back out.

3. The culture of people in poor communities is not different in its functioning from the culture anywhere else: it draws on a partly real, partly imagined past, and it imagines a variety of potential futures—both inspiring and cautionary—to inform current practices that meet individual and collective

needs. The difference is that the culture of poor communities exists under attack from a dominant culture that consistently uses violence—symbolic and literal—to maintain its dominance.

4. The most important legitimacy is the legitimacy of our own community as we come to define it for ourselves in collective struggle for freedom and more life. Attempts to impose a system of credentials from outside a poor community necessarily lead to falsehoods; few people in more privileged places believe the credentials anyway, and they do not understand our intention to raise our children to be literate, naturally self-sustaining inheritors and inventors of our own culture. Nevertheless, a well-developed and explicit basis for indigenous legitimacy *within* our community has the effect of building power in relation to other communities.

The foundation of a national network of youth-led enterprises can be built on the first two strengths in the list: *Pay young people to teach each other, using funds that the state appropriates for education.* It is clear that adolescents, especially in stressed communities, learn a great deal from their peers. There are, of course, relatively basic things that young people teach each other: how to keep up with the latest fashions, what music to listen to, how to do a dance or play a video game or get to a party. But much of what young people learn from each other is at quite an advanced technical level: how to negotiate overlapping social networks; how to manage stressful family responsibilities, often quite beyond more middle-class expectations of adolescent abilities; how to find and keep a part-time job; how to run some kind of independent money-making enterprise (not only selling drugs but also producing and promoting events, performing music or poetry, cutting hair, inking tattoos, or selling snacks, clothes, or bus passes). Young people not only learn how to do these things by trial and error but also share what they know with their friends and relatives, almost all of it informally.

Many young people also learn complex skills through interactions with adults outside of regular school hours. There are formal interactions in school-sponsored, church-sponsored, or neighbor-hood-based clubs, teams, and organizations; and there are informal but educational interactions with older friends, relatives, relatives of friends, and other neighborhood adults.

The point is this: young people in poor neighborhoods are very good at both teaching and learning—as we should expect, because they are human—they just don't learn much in schools. The problem isn't them; it's school. But the money earmarked to educate young people doesn't go to the people who actually teach them things—their peers and networks of neighborhood and family adults who care about them. The money goes into schools, and then flows right through and out of each poor community to somewhere already wealthier.

The relation of crime and violence to miseducation and poverty must be understood in this context. Literally billions of public dollars are spent in Baltimore each year on education, policing, and incarceration. Someone earns that money. But qualifying to earn public dollars requires some kind of successful track record of education and employment—a decent résumé—which is precisely what many people in poor communities don't have. The alternative, to survive, is to join underground and/or criminal economies, and children begin to hook into those economies from about fourth grade on. The billions of dollars in public money that should sustain the economy of poor communities ends up in the bank accounts of the credentialed classes, mostly people from outside the targeted communities. Eventually, the great bulk of public funds circulates in suburbs, not in inner cities, not on reservations, not in rural backwaters. For people in poor communities who are left without enough money to survive, life becomes even harder.

Their friend was dead. They sat around the Algebra Project office on couches and chairs and on the floor, mostly listening to Leon tell stories in his impossibly fast way of speaking about what he, Deonte, and David used to do growing up. Playing in the halls in middle school. At Leon's grandmother's house listening to music and rapping. The night Leon and Deonte got robbed up at Morgan State. Deonte got away, but Leon and the boy who tried to rob them were fighting. Skinny little Leon was so angry he ended up winning the fight, and when the police arrived, he was pummeling the boy, so the police arrested Leon. They didn't believe a word he said—crazily fast—about how he was the victim, not the criminal. But he's double jointed, or his wrists are so thin, or something, and he kept escaping from the handcuffs and would start to run, and the police would catch him again and again, till they finally chained him to a pole.

But this time Deonte didn't get away. Shot in the head waiting for the bus at the end of the alley by Jay's house, because he didn't have any money to give the robber, with David standing right beside him. They were coming from an Algebra Project meeting about fighting for youth jobs so teenagers wouldn't decide to sell drugs or rob people when they were hungry.

Qualifications and Accountability

A question arises: Which teenagers have the capacity to teach advanced subjects at the high school level? This is a question about the deficits in culture and legitimacy that are assumed to plague poor communities. Here is how we answer it: Young people in poor communities can create—and have already created—learning cultures at a high level of technical sophistication when structures are in place to buy their time and protect their individual and collective autonomy. It doesn't happen all at once, because schooling has to be unlearned. But the national Algebra Project and Young People's Project networks, for example, have had the experience of watching ordinary groups of high school students develop into competent mathematicians by working with slightly older peers who have some mathematical expertise to start with. The near-peers' time is bought by paying a decent wage adding up to anywhere from $5,000 to $10,000 a year for about two hours' teaching a day. They learn through training and experience how to teach by asking questions, and they model how to formulate and test conjectures and theories. These near-peers create powerful relationships with the slightly younger students and come to the classroom as living examples who have stepped onto an economic ladder not through knowledge of the drug trade but through knowledge of math.

This culture of math learning builds on the young people's own cultural strengths, and especially on the strength of looking out for each other in the face of adversity—a strength shared by adolescent cultures everywhere and prominent in the African American cultural tradition especially. School and the motivational structures of capitalism tend to overwhelm and obfuscate this strength in contemporary America. But when such a culture is fostered, it is very powerful. We recognize this, for example, in the context of team sports; "I'm only in it for myself" doesn't go very far on a football or baseball field. The testing, ranking, grading, and tracking that take place in schools undo the proclivity of young people under stress to want to look out for each other. Peer and near-peer teaching practice deliberately supports that proclivity and develops the idea that students are moving toward technical mastery—both individually and together.

Schooling always has and always will create boundaries between the "educated" and the "uneducated." That is the reason for schooling; it constructs an inside and an outside, places of inclusion in the power structure and places of exclusion from the power structure. So-and-so "speaks proper English," and so-and-so doesn't. Person A was accepted into college, but Person B never graduated from high school; therefore, Person A is entitled to more property and even to more life than Person B (the doctors at the Johns Hopkins Hospital live, on average, fifteen years longer than the residents of the community that immediately surrounds the hospital).[4] These artificial boundaries encourage policymakers to assume that poor communities do not have enough people who can teach what poor children need to learn. People in poor communities are "uneducated" by definition.

If an educational practice delimits one part of our people from another, it has no place in our parallel structure. And this insight is at the root of the idea to pay young people to teach each other. They know enough to construct knowledge individually and collectively. But they have not yet fully participated in the process of schooling, and so they have not yet become divided from their peers. By compensating them for their effort to maintain the integrity of the peer group, which is actually the integrity of the community, we disassociate the key weapon of the dominant society—cash—from the false teaching that you must have a credential to be paid. That false teaching, the credentialing system, is the mechanism for preserving caste adapted to the age of "democracy." We should no longer defer to it.

But the credentialing system has ironically opened up its own crawl space. Since *Brown v. Board of Education*, the strategy of "democratic" "equal opportunity" stratification by evaluating "merit" and then rewarding the more meritorious classes has led to unsustainable inequalities. An unintended result of these inequalities is that any adult who grows up in a poor neighborhood and achieves some kind of certifiable "merit" will likely take their skills to some other more comfortable and more rewarding jurisdiction to put them to use. But this leaves a "teacher shortage" back in the ghetto. Consequently, few adults who are both indigenous and certified are left in poor communities, and it almost seems reasonable to agents of the dominant culture to pay young people for instruction (for example, in algebra). As a result of the misconceptions that abound regarding education, merit, and certification in poor communities, an economic opening—a crawl space—becomes available for young people to offer what they know to their peers for a wage.

Twenty- to Thirty-Year-Olds

The parallel political economy of youth-led enterprises imitates the allure of gangs. One reason young people are attracted to gangs is that they offer a sense of belonging, a tradition of symbols and rituals that seems likely to continue. Gangs also structure employment and potential career ladders, as well as emotional support and physical protection. Existing peer-to-peer enterprises like the Baltimore

Algebra Project compete with gangs by creating a positive option for young people in struggle.

The upper reaches of the career ladder in these alternative gangs are already a dynamic source of social transformation. When young people have grown up in the context of a vibrant youth-controlled enterprise that helped to meet many of their social, emotional, political, and economic needs, by the time they are in their twenties they are noticeably bold, pragmatic, and astute. They have acquired social and cultural capital from the bottom up. These young adults, having achieved their goals not through the privileges of caste status but through the experience of making new, better arrangements for themselves individually and collectively, are now able to reinterpret the world as plastic and transformable rather than as monumental and immovable. They no longer experience dominant social, political, and economic structures as definitive and themselves as insignificant or powerless. They experience the larger structures as contextual or scenic and themselves as actors and writers of their own lives.

This twenty- to thirty-year-old cohort supplies a valuable perspective to thriving enterprises of many kinds. Adolescents are still inexperienced in considering wider contexts; often they display highly developed skills but have trouble seeing very far over the horizon. When they are just a little older, they better understand the relationship between their own actions and both the natural world and the human world and so effect more dynamic change in that larger world. These are the twenty-something athletes who break out in professional sports, emerging actors, musicians, and filmmakers; they are the military captains and lieutenants whose leadership inspires teenage recruits to advance on their enemies; and they are parents with young families, the most dynamic phase of parenthood and the one that requires the most energy. The leaders of SNCC, CORE, SDS, and the Black Panthers were of this age too.

Currently in poor communities, young adults in their twenties are for the most part either idle or blunted by mindless, routinized jobs—stocking shelves, working cash registers, flipping burgers, pacing around richer, whiter settings as security guards. There is no pool of capital to invest in them, and they are uncertain of their own abilities and virtues. However, young people who have grown up in peer-to-peer organizations are different: they are skilled, confident, and energetic. All they lack is capital and a larger structure through which to deploy their talent—like athletes without teams, dancers with neither troupe nor audience.

> Roger Taney's name is inscribed with the other chief judges of Maryland in the circular frieze of the ornate courtroom in Baltimore where youth charged as adults are brought for hearings on whether their cases will be waived back to the juvenile system. In 1857 the same Roger Taney wrote the *Dred Scott* opinion for the Supreme Court of the United States in which seven justices agreed that "the black man has no rights the white man is bound to respect."
>
> A century and a half later, the Baltimore courtroom is filled to hear the waiver motions of an Algebra Project student member who has been arrested and charged with armed robbery. Everyone in the courtroom is Black except the prosecutor, the defense attorney, and three teachers who have come to support TS. The courtroom is packed with Algebra Project youth leaders and college debaters, since TS is also a popular and charismatic member of Baltimore's Urban Debate League. The bailiffs are nervous about the crowd and insist that those who have no space to sit must wait in the hall outside.
>
> The stakes are high. An armed robbery conviction in the adult system would lead to a permanent record of felony and to a sentence served in the Maryland Penitentiary. In the juvenile system, sentences are served at a youth detention center, and juvenile records are, in theory, sealed.
>
> The twenty-year-old leaders of the Algebra Project, the teenage tutors, and a support group of adults have been meeting for weeks to plan for this hearing. They are organizers, so they pack the courtroom. But before TS's case is heard, several other waiver motions are on the docket. Boys in handcuffs and shackles are brought in, but they have

no supporters to testify that they should be treated as boys. Judge Davis, a mother herself (as she tells the courtroom), denies their motions one after the next. In each case, she delivers a stern lecture, explaining that given the nature of the charges, the strength of the evidence, and the reports of the social workers warning that the boys are disconnected from family, school, and community, she cannot in good conscience allow them to be treated as boys.

When TS is brought in, his attorney begins by asking everyone in the room to stand who is there to show their support for him. Fifty people rise, mostly young people, and the attorney mentions that there are more in the hall outside. He then calls witnesses to testify to TS's powerful work in the Algebra Project and the debate league. The judge also hears from the prosecutor and the social workers about the seriousness of the charges and the dislocations of TS's family, his school disciplinary record, and his truancy.

Finally, the judge pronounces: She has never before seen this kind of community support for a defendant youth charged as an adult. Sometimes a teacher or minister comes with parents and family. But she has never seen a group of activists like this in her courtroom. It is outside her experience. She does not quite understand what she is witnessing, but she feels that if she allows TS's case to be heard in the gentler environment of the juvenile system, she can be confident, at least, that he is attached to some network of community interest. It is the "lone wolves" who scare her—the boys who believe they must look out for themselves, because no one else will.

Redirecting Capital Flows

Where exactly will the students' wages come from in the parallel peer-to-peer economy? In the short run, teachers, organizers, and young people will have to look to philanthropy, to existing youth-workforce government programs, and to relatively small contracts with school systems and other public agencies for initial funding, as youth-led organizations do now. In Baltimore we are trying to create a pool of working capital from those sources that will let a small network of community-based youth-centered organizations expand their reach. Progress toward this goal is being made through a city charter amendment that directs roughly $12 million a year to various youth programs, some portion of which goes to peer-to-peer enterprises. A thoughtful grassroots process for distributing this money has been put in place by Leaders of a Beautiful Struggle, working through the mayor and city council. Rather than allowing the funds to slip away toward the nonprofit industrial complex, an assembly of self-selected local residents awards grants to community-based groups that do not need to produce shiny presentations and proposals.[5] They just need to show that there are already young people who want to work with them.

But at the scale of a whole city or county, we will need much more than these relatively small funding sources. To create employment in peer-to-peer knowledge work for thousands of young people in Baltimore, for example, we need access to a significant part of the state's and city's current operating budgets. Four or five years from now we may be talking about using 10 percent of the public money spent on education, policing, and juvenile incarceration. In Baltimore this is about $200 million a year, enough to create ten to twelve hours a week of employment for every high school student in the city. There would still be $60 million left over to hire twenty-to-thirty-year-olds to help maintain the youth-centered structure of community-based peer-to-peer enterprises.

Of course there are constituencies that already lay claim to that $200 million. But those constituencies are not the people that the schools, police, and juvenile incarceration budgets are said to serve. The budgets are purported to serve young people. So why not pay the young people to serve themselves? On the face of things, it makes sense that putting $200 million in the students' own pockets might be a better use of 10 percent of the youth service budgets than giving it to a set of institutional players who almost everyone acknowledges has failed.

The neoliberal argument is that public functions like education and policing should be privatized for the sake of economic efficiency. Our argument is that functions not administered by the people directly affected are not actually public; they are colonial, regardless of whether the administration is governmental, quasi-governmental, or private. Rather than moving from neocolonial government functions to neocolonial private functions, we should test the effects of genuine investment in the indigenous community, controlled by that community.

Making sense, of course, is not the same as having power. Wrestling hundreds of millions of dollars away from the interests currently profiting from ineffective educational and carceral programs will necessitate major campaigns involving thousands of committed people, led by youth. And, in the meantime, networks of peer-to-peer youth enterprises can be structured to develop the organizing power needed for this kind of campaign.

The great advantage of youth enterprises is the culture of self-reliance that they grow. Young people learn to define problems, structure solutions, and do the work needed to implement those solutions. They also learn nondeferential attitudes toward people who stand in their way, and they learn to surmount obstacles between them and their goals. In the course of this work, they gather support around them from older people and people from other communities. There are scores of historical examples of young people initiating social transformation: runaway slaves; the liberation movements of Africa, South America, and Asia; the current mobilizations of immigrant youth in the United States; the Movement for Black Lives.

The organizing campaigns that we are preparing will grow out of youth workplaces, drawing on historical parallels from both the Black freedom struggle and the labor movement. In the industrial age, contests over economic and political power centered on places where industrial goods were produced and distributed: in mines and factories, railroads and dockyards. Today, the fight is located where knowledge is produced and distributed. This is one of the reasons that universities have become battlegrounds. And it is also one of the reasons that public education has developed into a focal point for political and economic contention. Knowledge work creates profit centers. Educational services corporations extract billions of dollars each year from international education markets; and the education labor force is in tremendous flux, both because of attacks on unions and because some teaching functions have been automated through computer platforms—strategies for increasing corporate profits by reducing labor costs.

Peer-to-peer enterprises function as the modern equivalent of shop floors: they are labor intensive; they are geographically rooted in actual neighborhoods; and people participate in them face-to-face. The wage draws student workers, and in coming together to undertake knowledge work, young people make themselves available to develop political and educational consciousness, the way union workers in factories or dockyards used to do.[6]

Even on our small scale, we have found that once students experience the autonomy and empowerment of earning a wage, sharing what they know under the auspices of a youth-determined collective, they do not casually relinquish the opportunity. They fight to maintain their involvement, and many of them fight to expand the opportunity for friends and relatives. Their parents, grandparents, ministers, and neighbors respect both the young people's positive engagement and also the sponsoring organizations that make the employment possible. This support dramatically expands the organizing base.

Our calculation in Baltimore is that several years of philanthropic funding supplemented by relatively small public contracts will allow a network of youth enterprises to create an organizing base of several hundred young people, backed by their families. A thousand more young people who are being led in knowledge work by these paid youth leaders will also become invested in the strategy, enjoying the benefits of the youth-led activities and looking for similar work for themselves.

The political pressure created by this organizing base—together with the evidence of the excitement about and the learning that takes place through these knowledge-producing programs—will create momentum for a major demand-driven campaign: Direct a significant portion of education, police, and juvenile justice budgets to build out peer-to-peer youth enterprises. Award academic credit for demonstrated performance by students not only in school classrooms but also in school- or community-based enterprises. The portfolio assessment structure of the New York Performance Standards Consortium has already demonstrated the feasibility of attaching academic credit to student performance in this way. We are only adding the idea that community-based enterprises can be "cost centers" for delivery of academic services just as well as schools can.

Ten percent of these city and state youth services budgets may be initially beyond the reach of such a campaign, but 2 percent or 3 percent may be possible within just a few years. We envision aggressive campaign tactics: students, teachers, and families boycotting schools, setting up people's classrooms in communities where young people demonstrate that they can teach each other more effectively than the schools are doing—until authorities agree to redirect funding from, say, testing and professional development or drug testing and curfew patrols to youth employment in peer-to-peer enterprises.

Young people are the power in schools. They are able to block whatever they don't like by simply refusing to do what they are told or "malingering," as it used to be called. But their power has largely been diffuse and disorganized. Youth enterprises, like labor unions, are settings for learning about power and how to use it. The goal is not only to block the projects of the educational authorities but to change financial, administrative, and political arrangements so that young people's educational projects can get off the ground.

Or the strategy could be framed in this way: Communities should control their own education, but community-controlled education will be initiated by adolescents. Their dangerous energy has been a problem for every culture that has ever existed. Adolescent energy has to be contained and bounded but also supported to stimulate and spur new creation. Our society has separated these two tasks—containment and stimulation—and projected them onto two distinct populations of adolescents: young people of color and young people in poverty must be contained and bounded; privileged young people are stimulated and spurred. In contrast, the structure of youth enterprises has evolved to stimulate young people in poverty so that they can create their own boundaries and formalisms, leading their communities to take control of how the next generation of children grows up. Young people deploying their dangerous energy in an organized way are always frightening to established authority. Nevertheless, their leadership is the way forward for education in a democracy.

The young people of the Baltimore Algebra Project have held open leadership meetings almost every Friday for fifteen years. We envision similar institutionalized citywide youth assemblies of participants in the whole network of peer-to-peer enterprises. Such assemblies, perhaps modeled on the People's Movement Assemblies of the World Social Forum, can create a political culture of direct democracy and action that will have a real effect on how young adults see themselves as they emerge into political maturity. People's Movement Assemblies are a structured process to build consensus and develop action plans, emerging originally in Latin American efforts of the 1990s to oppose neoliberal globalism. The methods of the assemblies were diffused through the United States by the Occupy movement following the global economic collapse of 2008.

Young people who take part in people's assemblies tend not to see themselves as passive objects for politicians' commercials but as actors deciding their own course. They see themselves this way because of their experiences, ideas, and representations, because of how it feels to be an actor rather than an object, and because of the power that is acknowledged by a wider public that finds itself reacting to the students' autonomous structures. A substantial subset of young people in Baltimore and elsewhere has already experienced and started to make use of this power. These students are already operating beyond theory, in the domain of praxis.

Daysha had been tutoring for about a month after school in the library. She was thrilled to have the job. A little more than a hundred dollars every two weeks paid for her phone, some food, and some clothes. Her mother was proud, and her older sister was jealous. Daysha also realized that when she taught certain equations to ninth graders, she understood the equations better herself. She even began to raise her hand in math class, something she had never done before.

But today she was told to go downtown with two of the more experienced tutors. The tutors took turns representing their school site at the Friday meeting, which was held every week in some kind of office that she had heard the students ran themselves. When she walked in, she felt strange. Of course, she knew the other people from her school. They traveled down together so there had been no problem knowing where to go. But this office wasn't what she was expecting. There weren't any White people, no one "professional" looking, only Black teenagers, and a couple of older students who looked like they were in their twenties. Before the meeting began, the office was loud: greetings, cussing, horseplay, jokes. Someone was watching a video on the big screen. People lounged on sofas. It looked like someone was asleep under a blanket on a chair in the corner. There was pizza and soda, and everyone helped themselves. There were also some cluttered office desks, computers, printers, and a whiteboard covered in diagrams or numbers or arrows or equations—she couldn't quite tell what.

After a while, people started sitting down around the big tables in the center of the room, about twenty or twenty-five students in all, boys and girls, until one girl who looked like she might also be in the tenth grade said it was time to get started. The room calmed down. Daysha noticed just one or two people still looking at their phones, but soon they put them away.

One by one, each student was asked to say their name and their favorite snack to eat when binge-watching a TV show after midnight. Some people were answering straight, some were making jokes and coming up with weird things, like "bacon and eggs," and then everyone would jump in and play-argue back and forth for a while. When it was her turn, she felt awkward, because they were all looking at her, but she got through it: "Daysha, popcorn." Someone asked what flavor popcorn, and she answered, "Just regular, butter." They nodded and went on to the next person.

People started reporting about things. Different students would say how the tutoring sites were going, or that the assistant principal at one school was giving them a hard time for working at the site even when the teacher sponsor had to leave early. If there was no adult, they were supposed to just go home. But Alisha was eighteen, so she was an adult. Why couldn't they still work? Someone advised taking the problem to the principal, but someone else thought that would just make it worse, and it was agreed to simply ignore the assistant principal, who usually didn't find out till after the fact that they had gone on working even though the teacher had left early.

Then there were financial reports and reports on meetings that people had gone to, but Daysha couldn't really understand what the meetings were about, even though everyone else seemed to know. They were using all kinds of words she had never heard before, or at least never heard kids using: "memorandum of understanding," "pedagogy," "convergence." It was strange, too, that even though they seemed so intelligent, they talked regular. They didn't even use proper English all the time—she heard a lot of "ain't" and slang, like when they were deciding to ignore the assistant principal by saying, "She be bluffin'." Most of the students seemed confident about what they were reporting, going on and on about a whole lot of information. She tried to follow but would have had to interrupt every ten seconds if she was going to ask enough questions to understand.

When the reports were over, the girl who was facilitating said that Jamie had a proposal. Someone said Jamie should have sent the proposal out in an email before the meeting, because that was a policy. Jamie said her phone was off, and she couldn't send it out. The first person said she should have used a computer at school or something. The discussion went back and forth, until finally the facilitator called for a vote on whether Jamie could make her proposal this week or would have to wait till next Friday. "All in favor of Jamie making her proposal today, raise your hands. . . . All opposed? . . . Abstentions?" The vote was nineteen to three with one abstention, and Jamie started making her proposal. Daysha just kept her hand down the whole time, because she wasn't even sure if she was allowed to vote, and she didn't know what was right anyway.

Jamie's proposal was about sleeping in the office. She thought people should be allowed to spend the night in the office if they had nowhere else to go. There was a big discussion—not loud for the most part—but very serious. Daysha could tell some people were angry and some people were scared, and whichever way the proposal was decided, one side or the other was going to be upset. The problem seemed to be that several students had been sleeping regularly in the office, and an adult from another office in the building had reported them to the landlord. The landlord was kind of cool in general, according to the students, but he was a White man and sometimes pissed people off, and he charged too much rent anyway. They were afraid he might kick them all out, because tenants weren't allowed to use the office for residential purposes. One girl named Talia made a long speech about sleeping in her car, and a creepy man had seen her and knocked on the car window and then asked her if she wanted to go to his house for the night. Her speech was about how she felt much safer in the office and how she was trying to save up money for a security deposit so she could move into her own apartment, but in the meantime, she just needed somewhere safe to be.

It seemed that there was also a girlfriend involved, even

though no one said it straight out, and part of the problem was that Talia wanted to be with her girlfriend at night. But there were other students, too, who had slept at the office when their mothers put them out or because their heat was off at home. And then one of the older students talked about White supremacy and patriarchy and how housing was always an issue for Black people, especially for LGBTQ Black people and how the Algebra Project had a bigger bank account (most of the time) than any of the members, so if the organization could afford to pay the rent and keep the lights on, then why shouldn't students who were homeless use the office as a place to stay when they needed to?

In the end everyone agreed to wait till next week to make a final decision, and one of the older students was going to talk to the landlord to make sure he calmed down in the meantime.

As the meeting was breaking up, a boy came over and asked Daysha if she had a way to get home. She said her mother was coming to get her, and another boy came over and asked her if she had a sister named Lisa in the eleventh grade at Western. Daysha suddenly realized this was the boy her sister was talking to on Instagram. She asked him why he wanted to know, but he had a good comeback, and as they joked together for a minute, she decided to try to get Lisa to come down to the office with her next Friday. Coming here was fun, and maybe Lisa could get a job here too.

CHAPTER 3

Building Capacity

When I began teaching in Baltimore public schools—August 28, 1987—I soon came to understand that to teach, I would also have to learn how to organize. My family had emigrated to Canada from Ohio in 1968, afraid that my brother and I would be swept up in the Vietnam draft, though we were only ten and eleven at the time. Returning to the United States in the '80s, I knew nothing of American public schools, let alone schools that only Black students attended. There were a number of outstanding teachers and administrators at Walbrook High School, since closed, but I was shocked by what students appeared to accept as "education." The African American school librarian locked up all the books that students wanted to read—largely Black history and Black literature—in a small forbidden closet, never lending out a book, because she said the students who borrowed books wouldn't return them, and she was afraid her collection would disappear. Eighteen-year-old men and women would be reduced to tears standing at attention in the White English department head's office while he debated with himself whether he would approve their twelfth-grade English credit or deny them a passing grade, their last hurdle before achieving a high school diploma. He explained to me that the students' parents were concerned not that their children learned to write effectively or to read challenging material but only that they would know to obey a White man when he told them what to do, so they would be successful in the world of work.

The student despair at Walbrook High School and the dismal educational effects that were obvious results of injustice caused me unintentionally to look at things as an organizer. When I came across Bob Moses and the Algebra Project in 1995 and read his article called "Organizing in the Spirt of Ella,"[1] the connection between organizing and teaching was made explicit. This chapter explores some of the lessons that teachers can learn, once we see ourselves as organizers.

How to Build a Successful Youth Enterprise

Teacher/organizers will want to understand how to support the development of peer-to-peer enterprises. A healthy peer-to-peer youth enterprise must have four characteristics: First, it must be youth-determined. Some people are comfortable with total youth control. Some want adults in authoritative roles for stability, security, and financial management. Whatever the actual governance structure, the young people must be convinced that they have the power to determine what takes place in the organization, both in the larger plans and directions and also in the operational details. Virtually all the institutions of the United States, public and private, teach the incapacity of the young. Therefore, to be convincing, youth-determined spaces must err in the direction of too much youth power, not too little. When there is a serious disagreement between young people and older people, the young should prevail, except in cases of absolute danger. This is how young people decide whether they are actually empowered or only patronized.

Second, most of the young people involved must be paid significant wages. I am describing a parallel structure of education for communities that are fighting for survival. There is a cultural and spiritual dimension to survival, but there is also a material dimension. Our students need to eat. They need to get from one place to another. They need homes with electricity and water and heat. They need clothes and phones and a sense of dignity. They need not to be torn apart by anxiety about the tenuousness of any of these necessities, or at least they need to be in an environment that acknowledges the reality of their material anxiety by trying to address it with seriousness and consistency. They need a decent wage.

Third, the organization must be able to convey a sense of having a past that is worth preserving and a future that the current participants are helping to build. In other words, the organization must have a genuine culture, distinguishable from but intertwined with a larger encircling culture that may be defined in many different ways. We human beings derive our willingness to invest time and effort from the understanding of our transitional roles between the past and the future. These transitional roles are partly symbolic and partly literal. We share our grandmothers' genes. We also use her tablecloth on holidays because of its meaning to us. Our children will preserve and pass on something of us and of whatever was symbolically powerful in our lives. What is clear about families is also clear about peer groups (and about our interactions with near-peers, people just slightly older and slightly younger than ourselves): we work hardest when we feel we belong to something that existed before us and may exist after us if we all do our work well. Even groupings that seem to be brand new organizations are stocked full of symbols and ideas retrieved from some kind of lore or fertile past experience. The key is that the young people involved must be convinced of the value of this experience by how it feels in its present incarnation in them. Being told about its value is insufficient.

Fourth, there must be older adults around who affirm the young people's instincts and efforts, and the role of those adults must make sense to the young people. It is frightening to be free, and we are talking about freedom. Messing up is part of being free. But we are each alone and not alone. People acting freely in ethical ways feel responsible for their actions, but they also feel that others are with them, sharing the burden. Older people have a unique ability to encourage boldness and self-love in young people who are risking what might seem at the time to be everything. When young people feel that they have failed, we see that they have only stumbled and help them stand up again. We are eyes and ears, and we point in directions for them to experiment or be wary. We can embody a stability that gives young people the courage to stray far into new possibilities.

Young People Travel Together

Organizers must follow the lead of the people they are organizing. The social structures that youth make for themselves should be respected. For example, many young people travel together: groups that include siblings, cousins, friends, and teammates often act as units, not as separate individuals. Their connections to each other have little to do with their failures in the dominant education system, their academic track, or their status in the legal system. Youth enterprises accommodate this sociological characteristic. The younger sibling is invited into the enterprise, even though the design of the group is for older youth. An enterprise for homeless youth doesn't exclude a friend who lives with her parents.

This should be obvious: a community includes all the people in the community, not only some. But the current financial and bureaucratic structures of schooling and youth services violate these obvious norms. Most egregiously, certain youth funding streams are only for youth in designated zip codes, age ranges, or income brackets, interrupting vital peer or kinship bonds. In Baltimore, we learned this disruption concretely in 2008. After an intense youth-led organizing campaign that included camping for a week at City Hall and a hunger strike, funding for peer-to-peer youth enterprises to the tune of several million dollars emerged from a combination of private foundation and state government sources. But powerful officials decided that the funds should come through a structure that required participants to fit mandated categories: adjudicated youth and youth in foster care. Most of the grassroots youth-powered groups who had pushed for employment that they themselves could structure were excluded from decision-making roles. They weren't able to satisfy the state that they were providing services only to the designated categories and not incidentally to nonqualifying youth, even though the nonqualifying youth might be siblings or neighbors. The organizations that ended up with access to the funding were mostly adult-run bureaucratic nonprofits with zero youth-determined culture and insufficient stipends for the young people, instead of the full-blown autonomous youth enterprises originally pictured. The funding died out, having interrupted the indigenous, autochthonous constituency that had won the funding in the first place.

How to Organize

1. Listen. Ask questions to be sure you understand the problems and needs the young people are explaining.

2. Consider whether there is a structure (youth-powered or potentially youth-powered) that already exists through which the young people themselves could work to meet their need. If not, think about what elements that structure should have. Include youth wages.

3. Invite several young people into the structure—it doesn't need to be a lot—and then ask them to invite their peers, or invite them to create a new structure, if necessary.

4. Support them in the structure enough so that they are successful, at least to some extent.

5. Repeat, modifying formulations of the problem, structural elements, invitations to enter the structure, and support as necessary, only just enough.

All teaching and organizing—whether the teachers and organizers are older, near-peers, or peers—is on the boundary of "too much" and "too little." In supporting young people, organizers and teachers almost always do too much. This is disempowering for youth. But the tendency to do too much should not motivate teachers to do nothing. The organizer's or teacher's support is often crucial to the life of a youth organization. Without it, what might have been forward motion can become a long period of stagnation. Organizers do only what the target population cannot yet do for itself. Overbalancing is inevitable. We only find the right measure by noticing that we have gone too far or not far enough, noticing because something bad happens and enforces a correction.

But young people are able to do a great deal for themselves. For example, they can run meetings and participate effectively and productively in conducting the affairs of an organization. With practice, once a culture develops over several years, they become quite expert, and the culture starts to be passed along to the next generations.

Trusting young people's ability to manage themselves implies trusting their decisions. Sometimes an organizer or teacher can suggest—either inside or outside the meeting—a strategy, structure, or course of action that has not arisen yet from the group. Sometimes an organizer or teacher should bring the young people into contact with others—peers or older people—that they would not encounter otherwise, who could help move work along. Often organizers or teachers, in initial stages, should find some money to help build cohesion. Youth meetings often need a little bit of food and transportation to ensure that everyone can be present.

Older teachers and organizers working with youth organizations must recognize that young people are only truly empowered when they make decisions that the organizer or teacher thinks are mistakes but supports anyway. It would fall into the category of doing too much to block the students' decision since that would disempower them. Mistakes are good if we learn from them, and it often turns out that young people have insights adults misunderstand as mistakes. Of course, it would fall into the category of doing too little if the students make a mistake so disastrous that they can never recover. Mistakes on that scale, however, are much rarer than we think. We must be careful not to let our fear—especially fear about our own standing or reputation—get in the way of our judgment about the actual consequences of the young people's mistakes.

In 2014 the Baltimore City School Board was scheduled to vote on a number of school closings, including a school that had a substantial base of Algebra Project members. Without much preparation, students planned a meeting takeover to interrupt the vote. I thought their plan was a bad idea, and I told them so. They hadn't done their homework. There wouldn't be enough supporters present. The board was too far along in its process. The students were trying to expand their math teaching contracts, and this might alienate board members. And risking arrest can be a powerful tactic, but it comes with costs that I felt the students had not carefully thought through.

They went ahead anyway. I went with them, helping with rides and arranging some legal assistance if they needed it. As the school closing topic came up on the agenda, a dozen students began a die-in in front of the dais, shouting in unison, "I can't breathe!" The board members, upstaged, recessed and left the room, at which point the students occupied the members' seats and reconvened a people's meeting. The public audience responded with rousing support and passionate testimony. No one was arrested. In the end, though the takeover only delayed the board vote by a couple of hours, the power of the action as broadcast on the evening news galvanized public attention. Large unexpected donations came in. Collaborations began with several other activist groups that had witnessed the action. Debriefing and subsequent discussions added to the students' understanding of how a better-planned campaign could have leveraged the takeover tactic to create more power in the longer term. And most importantly, from my perspective, the students saw that their actions evoked responses from the people around them. The true audience of most organized actions is not the authorities but your peers—your own community—and even yourself; taking action, you and your peers come to understand yourselves as protagonists, not props or victims in someone else's drama. Supported in living freely, the students learned what would have been hard to learn any other way.

A good teacher does not stop a child from trying to climb a tree, even though they might fall. A good teacher does not often tell a student that their approach to a math problem is wrong; the student should usually try and see where it leads them. Sometimes they find a new way, and at least we can understand something of how they are thinking, how they are perceiving. A good organizer does not tone down students' demands, even when the demands are going to rile the authorities and maybe even alienate some supporters. By all means point out the possible effects of a strident tone and suggest alternatives if you feel the need. But the organizer's goal is not any particular tactical victory; the organizer's goal is that the target population understands its own power.

Against Walls

In a workshop I once heard José López Rivera of Chicago's Puerto Rican Cultural Center, adapting Mao, say that "the teacher gives back with precision what the students present in confusion." Adolescents both trust themselves and do not. To support the development of viable youth enterprises, adults must act in ways that build young people's collective confidence and treat their self-doubt as a product of oppression, a tool of the enemy, and so as something to be resisted at every turn.

There is a dilemma here: Teenagers can be impulsive. Their acting out can hurt them or hurt others. Learning to control impulses is an important part of growing up in any society. But a primary weapon of White supremacy and patriarchal exploitation is to implant almost physically an automatic hesitation in the minds of the exploited. For survival, people in oppression learn to defer to authority in public settings. But the survival mechanism often becomes a reflex in response to *any* formal challenge (an unconscious reaction), and as a reflex, it turns into self-doubt and hesitation. This reflex underlies the academic confusion often suffered by African-ancestored students in America. In formal settings, rather than take risks and look for adventures, our students doubt their own senses, observations, emotions, and thoughts, or relegate risk and adventure-seeking, enjoyment and trust to peripheral locations—alleys, corners, stairwells, hallways, the back row of class. Instead they should be encouraged to trust themselves, their senses, and their observations in formal settings, too, and good organizers or teachers do this by supporting rather than inhibiting, their impulses.

Distinguishing between good impulses and destructive impulses is a matter of attending to purposes. When my purposes are narrow and only immediate, I should perhaps hesitate (though even here, we risk inhibiting spontaneity). But when my purposes involve a principle, the collective, a question of justice, or the building of knowledge structures, I should trust my anger, joy, curiosity, and intelligence and move forward.

The oppressor builds walls: physical, psychological, metaphorical. Walls define property. Many oppressed people feel disdain for those definitions of property, and some find ways to turn that disdain to pragmatic use. But often the oppressor's walls leave the oppressed feeling powerless and property-less. There are boundaries that ethics dictates we all must respect, such as the boundary that delimits each individual, in some way, from any other. We should control our impulses when otherwise we will affront another *person*. But there is no ethical requirement to control our impulses when we are running up against a boundary that exists only to define an institution's unjust power over us, no ethical requirement when we come up against a wall.[2]

We who believe in freedom help children attend to the differences between illegitimate and legitimate boundaries or, in other words, to understand where legitimacy comes from. And in the process of learning about this difference, as they consciously begin to confront racism, capitalism, patriarchy, and war, adolescents naturally begin to formalize their collectives. Good teachers and good organizers encourage young people to trust their thoughts and feelings about exclusion and injustice. They also encourage young people to consider thoroughly their ethical obligations, to hesitate when a person's integrity—not their power to oppress—might be violated.

Consider the wall between students in poor communities and food. A great deal of confusion in schools of poverty comes from trouble around food: the chemistry of our students' bodies is out of balance, both chronically and also from hour to hour because of lack of access to healthy food and water during the school day. Students know they are hungry and thirsty; they feel the fogginess in their brains and the weakness in their limbs, and they know they are distracted because they need to eat.

But they don't think of themselves as having a collective right to eat and almost never organize themselves to solve the problem socially or politically. In almost every high school of poverty, students know who has a stack of junk food in their locker that they sell between periods. Some schools legitimize this practice by creating school stores that sell snacks, open on completely inadequate schedules, and the school stores themselves are less and less common the poorer the school population. But it is easy to imagine a legitimate food operation—a student enterprise that offers plentiful, healthy food on demand: fruit, salads, protein bars, soups, beans and rice, pasta. Rather than telling students to ignore or dismiss their hunger, teachers and organizers should validate the need for nourishment and reject all the boundaries and obstacles schools put in between students and nutrition. The arguments that they will make a mess or be distracted or walk out of class to get something to eat are excellent considerations, well within the capability of youth collectives to discuss, debate, and solve through their own formalisms. What should be completely unacceptable is the doctrine that operates within the walls of a school that children should distrust their own craving for nutrition.

We are urging teachers and organizers to take young people seriously both as individuals *and as collectives.* Of course, thousands of wonderful teachers get food to their students every day, or arrange transportation, or hook them up with jobs or with health care or counseling. We who believe in freedom understand what it is to take young people seriously as individuals. We need to add to that a disposition to see young people's relationships to each other as incipient collectives and a disposition to help them put these incipient collectives on a sound footing, either inside or outside of schools.

In many poor communities there are already adults who gather young people around them informally and sponsor various powerful activities. We want to build this process out with a little extra support. We do not accept the too-often-internalized message that our children are incapable of organizing themselves, of collaborating to get what they need.

Kat and Alanis

Katherine Engleman (B.S. in architecture, Morgan State University; master's in architecture, University of Pennsylvania; master's in landscape architecture, University of Pennsylvania) started working for the Algebra Project in Baltimore as a high school sophomore in 2007. She was a tutor, an organizer, and the business director for the organization, finally leaving the collective in 2014, when she moved to Philadelphia for graduate school. She became involved with Youth United for Change in Philadelphia, first as a volunteer and more recently as a paid organizer.

One of Kat's mentees is Alanis Brown, who, as of this writing, attends the Pratt Institute in New York City. Alanis first met Kat when she attended an Algebra Project study group as a middle schooler in 2013. Alanis worked for the Algebra Project for three years in high school and has kept in close contact with Kat since then. Some of their thoughts on how the Algebra Project affects young people are transcribed below.

Kat

The Algebra Project was my first job [in high school], so I think I'm in a relatively privileged position. I haven't had to work in fast food or service work without any particular meaning. I earned a pretty high wage to gain skills that are now useful for me in my organizing work and as a teacher. Having access to that was a rare opportunity and opened doors for a lot of reasons.

I developed skills as a teacher, and it's a framework that I have taken to all of my political education and organizing work, explaining concepts I would never have had if I hadn't had that job. Most people don't get the opportunity to be in positions of power in organizations till much later in life, but now I'm a twenty-six-year-old, and I can become an ED or build my own organization.

Alanis is a good example. We have a close relationship, and I think that for her, having people—particularly young Black women—invested in seeing her develop was a particularly powerful experience. I wasn't superconscious, like "Me, as a Black woman, I'm having this effect on another Black woman," but I can see how it was useful; having somebody like me who wanted to be in Alanis's life was helpful.

There are certain things that young people respond to when it comes from another young person as opposed to an adult. Young people have the ability to learn from their peers, and they want to hold one another accountable: "I want to share what I know with you. I want to help you develop" or "I want to see you become a leader in this organization."

For instance, there's an alternative school, and they did voter registration. I don't think I could have registered the corner boys to vote, but because one of those students knows them, they're in the same age range, and they have some similar experiences, he was taught about a subject, and then he was able to talk to his peers about why voting is important, what it means for their lives, in a way that an adult or somebody who doesn't have that same experience couldn't do.

Some schools teach you how to be a leader and make decisions, but the vast majority of schools, especially in working-class neighborhoods, don't teach you how to do that. They teach you how to follow rules to get a job. So the larger question is, How do you restructure not only schools but society so that people can make decisions about their lives, can be active protagonists?

Alanis

I can talk about Kat, because we connected through the pedagogy in the math tutoring. She really impacted me. She was completely unaware of certain things she told me about herself or what she does—I thought she was so cool, like a celebrity or something. She's gone from the organization, and I'm in college now, but I just visited her, and I think it just helps those relationships that we really need.

I think I cared more for her because not only is she a woman; she is still finding herself with a mixed identity, and I still have to find myself, even though my mom is Black and my dad is mixed, and I haven't felt like I fit in a lot, and to find somebody that's in the same job as me who could really relate and understand me, that *deepened my racial consciousness about the world too. She helped gear me about ways to think about myself in American society.*

The Algebra Project, being youth led, kind of got me in trouble. I'm very outspoken. I feel like I stand out from all my friends. I know the type of people I want to be around, having been in the Algebra Project environment. Math is not an easy subject, and I think it's really powerful when you have teenagers that are in this organization and run this organization also doing math. That changes how you think of yourself now and in the future. It empowers you. Being around my coworkers without adults, there would be some days when adults weren't there at all, and we still get work done, or facilitate meetings, or have other organizations come in, and afterwards—I wasn't the only person who felt like that—we were like, "Wow, we just facilitated a meeting, or we just spoke to this other organization and networked, and now they want to contact us."

You don't think of yourself as a child anymore. You think of yourself as an adult, and I said it can get me in trouble because my family is so constructed to say you're a child till you move out of the house and pay your own rent. But because of my education from the Algebra Project and how it influences my thoughts in the world, I don't think of myself as a child. I don't think I am. I still can't do everything I want to do, but my conscience and the way I process things is really mature and advanced.

Teachers Emerge from Community

Our work is *not* to help White teachers learn to teach students of color. The numerical dominance of White teachers in schools of poverty is a symptom or tool of oppression. Our work is to end White teachers' numerical dominance in the education of children of color.

Where will the teachers come from? They are already there in the schools: they are the students. Immediately, they could be employed both inside and outside schools to start teaching what they know to their peers. But peer teaching is also a long-term strategy for developing a corps of teachers who will educate the next generation. If we had expanded the work of youth enterprises ten years ago, there would already be thousands of Black, Latinx, Asian, and Indigenous twenty-somethings, two years out of college, available to teach in the neighborhoods where they grew up. But the path to teaching cannot be the path we have today. Students who will become teachers in a self-healing community cannot apprentice to the managers and foremen of an oppressive system. They cannot apprentice within the institutions that must be overthrown.

Instead, they should apprentice with the people in their communities who already love and teach them. Some of these teachers can be found in schools and crawl spaces, fighting to survive. Many are in crawl spaces outside of schools—in churches, on the street, in theaters, universities, gyms, libraries. Our work is to build a network of grassroots organizations that have the funding and capacity to buy the students' time by employing them in knowledge work. Growing up in these base communities, young people develop a vision of continuing in new roles as they mature, in effect becoming the next generation's teachers.

The surplus wealth of the nation is more than sufficient to underwrite such a project, even on a large scale. After all, the surplus wealth of the nation is sufficient to arrest, try, and imprison a huge segment of the very same population. What is lacking is not capital but a vision *in the young people themselves* of their potential role teaching the generation coming behind them. The youth enterprises I have been describing give young people that vision: they make new roles viable because they pay a wage and offer a path through experience into the future by helping students feel what it is like to be central actors in their own lives right now, as opposed to being told what they are being prepared for.

Teachers currently in schools, professors currently in colleges and universities, organizers currently in neighborhoods, policymakers, politicians, ministers, families, and young people themselves all need to articulate a vision of education with at least this one characteristic: People must take on the responsibility for educating the next generation of their own community, and the capacity to educate the next generation already resides in the community. No need to look elsewhere. I am not promoting isolation or separation. I am talking about who we believe is capable of teaching and learning. Each *liberated* neighborhood must educate its own children, and adolescents growing up must hear not only that they can learn but also that they can teach. We are organizing the young to build to a demand that they be allowed to teach, which means that, since they are poor in twenty-first-century America, they must be compensated for teaching.

The Benefits of Youth Employment

The earlier a person is hired in formal employment, the more likely they are to be continually employed in the future, with higher lifetime earnings and a lower chance of being unemployed at any particular time. They are also more likely to be married, less likely to be divorced, and less likely to be incarcerated.[3] It is easy to see why employment early in life results in social integration. Even a little bit of money earned as a teenager converts to immediate, highly tangible rewards: You can buy a snack or some clothes you like. You can go on a date. When you're with friends, you don't have to always feel broke and embarrassed. And you don't need to respond to offers to do something illegal or perform a sex act for a little cash or to get a meal. Just not pestering your parents for small sums of money can make things smoother with them, and sometimes you can even help out with the bills.

Early employment also imposes a schedule that distinguishes the routines of childhood from the responsibilities and freedoms of adolescence. Little kids go to school, come home, do their homework, go outside, watch TV or play video games, and go to bed. But working teenagers' schedules are different, because they have to fit a job into their day the way adults do. Looked at historically, the structure of adolescent time has not yet emerged from the agricultural and industrial eras, when teenagers could enter the workforce directly at age fifteen or sixteen. In the information age, obligated to attend school in a majority of states until age seventeen or eighteen, underqualified for most employment without a high school diploma, many teenagers are held in a kind of time limbo, babysat by the system when they are not at all babies. Currently teenagers work after school, but I will outline below an alternative plan in which the school/work/recreation balance might result in a whole different kind of schedule.

The Benefits of Worker Cooperatives

The worker-owned, worker-managed cooperative is a viable business model that generally demonstrates higher productivity and more stable employment than conventional business designs.[4] The key feature of worker cooperatives is that workers are not in roles subordinate to management but in fact share the management role among themselves. This leads to several concrete efficiencies, and it also strengthens workers' individual and collective identities as nondeferential vis-à-vis hierarchical authority.

One fascinating source of long-term efficiency in worker cooperatives is well documented[5]: When business slows for whatever reason, many cooperatives agree to reduce workers' pay across the board in order to avoid layoffs. Later, when business picks up, no time or money is wasted rehiring old employees or training new employees. Employee turnover is a major and sometimes debilitating expense in conventional restricted-ownership firms.

A similar cooperative dynamic has played out several times among the young people of the Baltimore Algebra Project. Because the workers themselves manage the organization and decide on compensation structures, it is likely that wages will be equitably distributed rather than inequitably weighted toward the people with the most credentials or connections. Seeing themselves more as a neighborhood than as a firm, the members conceive of the unit as indivisible. It has integrity in relation to the larger society. When this integrity is attacked from the outside, as when a powerful outside agent—a politician, a funder, an entrepreneur, even a girlfriend—makes a play for a star-quality member, offering money and power if the member will break with the group, the action is perceived, by the group, as a betrayal of the first order.

The strong sense of the integrity of the cooperative unit also creates an alternative understanding of property or an experience of property in a new context. In the typical capitalist firm, assets belong to the firm's owner. Labor is exchanged for a wage in a transaction that shifts cash from the employer to the employee. Workers may or may not identify their interests with the interests of the firm's owner. In contrast, children in a family own nothing. It is only at a certain age that children in their culturally specific contexts may begin differentiating between property that is "mine" and property that is "the family's." This understanding accelerates in adolescence in many cultures, especially in ours, as children begin to feel social and material pressure to earn their keep. Generally speaking, adolescents begin to acquire property that they see definitively as their own while still sharing the family's collective property.

The worker's relation to a cooperative is both similar to and different from a child's relation to a family and the employee's relation to a privately owned firm. As is true in a family, each individual in the cooperative has a communal relation to the organization's collective property. But as is true in a private firm, the role of each worker's labor is spelled out concretely in several ways: how much time is required; what tasks or duties will be performed; how the cooperative's resources will be shared based on a variety of internal and external factors.

This unique experience with property in cooperatives has many consequences, two of which are especially important here. First, this experience supports the exercise of democracy. Where there is a sense of collective ownership, there is a tendency for decisions to be made democratically.[6] At their best, the experience of property in worker cooperatives encourages the sharing of decisions and the distribution of authority. Workers can learn to pay attention to the needs and desires of coworkers; to ask questions in order to get a fuller understanding of those needs and desires; to be creative, proactive, and experimental about balancing or reconciling the various needs and desires of the group. Job-sharing—as opposed to layoffs—is one example of how cooperatives balance their members' needs and desires. Workers can also learn to represent their

particular views, argue and dispute with other workers, or form cau-
cuses without destroying the integrity of the collective. These abilities are crucial political methods in a democracy. But there are few
mainstream institutions in the United States today where such skills
can be regularly practiced.

Second, worker cooperatives generally lead to the emergence
of positive educational practices. There are, first, the skills that are
needed to perform the work of the enterprise. These are shared from
one member to another. For example, a young person who joins
a cooperative recording studio will learn recording techniques or
marketing or bookkeeping from more experienced members. But
the less hierarchical structure of cooperatives also inspires spontaneous experimentation, inquiry, and study. Similarly, wherever
workers succeed in developing craft guilds, labor unions, or collective control of workplaces, they develop reading circles, study
groups, and popular education techniques. Jessica Gordon Nembhard has documented scores of study groups emerging concurrently
with African American worker cooperatives. The modern university itself arose in tandem with the craft guilds of medieval France
and Italy. Lawrence Goodwyn reminds us that the "sub-alliance"
structure of the populist Farmers' Alliance of cooperatives in late
nineteenth-century America was considered by the participants as
a "schoolroom."[7]

Conceiving ourselves as subordinates, we will take direction
from someone more elevated in the social hierarchy. Conceiving
ourselves as equals, we must find our own direction in collaboration with our peers. But to find our own direction, we need to know
more about the terrain—where we have come from, where we are
going, and what vehicles are at our disposal or how we might improve on them. This need provokes new learning.

All Learning Is Contextual

This is, of course, the way all knowledge has been or ever will be
generated: ideas develop as answers to problems that confront ordinary human beings in concrete circumstances. Someone proposes

an idea; they and others explore it, test it, elaborate on it, modify it; if it's useful, they communicate it to others who might confront a similar problem in their own concrete circumstances. The absurd codification of "standards" guiding what students must know and be able to do perverts the role of knowledge by pretending that there are useful ideas independent of the problems we face. But there are none. There are useful generalizations which may have been arrived at in one context and that nevertheless can be applied to many concrete problems in different contexts. That is a beautiful fact about the world. But those generalizations only have force in application.

The stimulation of confronting the world, or cooperating with the world, to accomplish purposes that arise in the course of living is far better motivation than grades. Many successful educational programs engage the world directly, and everyone understands that they are helpful. Youth Build is an organization through which young adults face the challenge of rehabbing houses. Outward Bound has decades of success in bringing young people from all walks of life to overcome challenges found in nature—hiking, rock climbing, or canoeing. We understand that school- and club-sponsored athletics instill discipline and a sense of teamwork and accomplishment. Young people don't engage in these challenges for a grade. The accomplishment and the reward are the same thing.

Needless to say, young people in poverty face plenty of obstacles without being taken out to a remote mountainside and left to find their way to safety. What is different about an educational or recreational program is that the challenge is structured to improve chances for success. This is how many—though not all—young people in wealthier families experience adolescence: tough in some respects, possibly very challenging, sometimes disappointing, but structured to improve chances of success. The informal structures around young people in poverty, however, are much less helpful. So social service agencies and nonprofits create their own programs—temporary structures for some subset of poor youth designed to create experiences that feel relatively successful. Very few programs of this kind, however, change the underlying dynamic of oppression. We are proposing something more than a program, less than a full-scale revolution. It is an ecosystem on the scale of a neighborhood with sufficient material, political, social, and cultural structure to shift community perception and self-perception about who are viable actors on the public stage. This ecosystem becomes a platform for what may develop, in struggle, into a fuller and more sudden reordering of power.

Nothing tangible stands in the way of the indigenous economic and educational developments that I and other organizers are envisioning. The difficulty lies entirely in the relationship structures we decide to foster. Battles must be fought with forces of oppression, certainly. But those battles will take place concurrently with the establishment of healthier relationships within our communities. Patterns of relationship can be imposed top-down, but those are usually destructive patterns that force someone "below" to respond to someone "above." But patterns of relationship can also be developed in mini-societies that evolve a collective culture, guided initially, perhaps, by those who have indigenous authority in the community, and then shifting toward fuller autonomy in a process that mirrors adolescence emerging into adulthood.

Youth-to-Adult "Professional Development"

One stage in the transition I am describing occurs when groups of students begin regularly teaching teachers how to deliver lessons, engage with young people, and explore new methods of understanding what has been learned. There is no reason "professional development" funds in the hundreds of millions of dollars should be paid to experts from outside rather than to the students themselves.

Once a group of young people figures out how to learn something, they can also figure out how to teach it. And if they can teach it to other young people, they can also teach it to adults. Take a literature topic, for example. Some teenagers may have come across Viet Thanh Nguyen's novel *The Sympathizer*, a deep analysis of American colonial violence and the Vietnam War—the whole work drawing significantly from Ralph Ellison's *Invisible Man*. Students may introduce this text to their peers through a youth-run enterprise using a variety of techniques: films, debates, role plays, visiting speakers, and written responses (poems, plays, essays). The reading may branch out into finding parents or community members who have oral, written, or photographic histories to contribute on the Vietnam War—as American soldiers or as antiwar resisters or as Vietnamese immigrants or their ancestors. Maybe some of the youth organizers' peers read the entire novel. Maybe some only read the first part, and maybe others read excerpts. The group may put on a public event to share its work with the neighborhood, celebrating the novel and their collective research. This kind of intense reading, research, and sharing goes on in crawl spaces in and out of schools all across the country already.

What we are adding is the idea that such research, appreciation, and sharing should become the normal paid labor of peer-to-peer enterprises. The next step is for the school system to contract with these enterprises so that they can share their curriculum and resources with teachers. A team of five to ten high school students, supported, maybe, by a college-aged mentor, could present their work to twenty or thirty teachers on a regular professional development day. They could present a clip of oral history from one of their neighbors and discuss the questions and process they used to elicit their neighbor's narrative. They could share critical articles about the book that they found useful and historical materials that helped them build context. And the school system could pay the young people for this collaboration. Projects like this one are well within our grasp right now.

I am emphasizing the economic arrangement, but the underlying issue is the total educational act. Young people engaged in this kind of work are learning many things all at once. They are learning to read and analyze. They are learning history. They are learning to communicate their ideas orally and through various media. They are learning about their community. They are learning that they can make things happen. They are learning about the supply of a knowledge-based product and about the demand for it. They are learning about contracts and wage structures. And they are learning how to overcome obstacles, because there will certainly be obstacles.

They may also develop a critical approach to current American colonial policies and may decide to engage in political questions that have both local and worldwide ramifications.

A project my colleagues and I are working on now is to develop a cadre of high school students in Baltimore who will train teachers in a new approach to teaching calculus. As things stand, careers in science and technology are beyond the reach of 90 percent of students of all backgrounds because first-year college calculus filters them out. The problem is even more severe for African American and Latinx students. The Algebra Project believes that traditional introductions to calculus are unnecessarily complex, and we have taught key concepts effectively to unexceptional math students in high school using very simple ideas from eighth grade algebra and geometry.[8] There is nothing conceptual that stands in the way of vastly improving the transition to college calculus. What stands in the way is a sociological and economic issue: we want to direct a change in calculus pedagogy from the bottom up by beginning with cadres of high school students *as instructors of teachers* rather than by beginning with college professors and moving from the top down. College professors certainly appreciate the subtleties of calculus more deeply than the students, and those insights will be welcome at higher levels of study, but the students have pedagogical insights that are more relevant to other students who are just beginning to learn the same material.

Reparations and Indigenous Authority

There are literally thousands of examples of indigenous educational and economic development in poor communities around the world, and yet, generally speaking, these communities continue to be starved of capital. Sometimes microcapital is enough to start a successful enterprise; sometimes it is not enough. The Nobel laureate Muhammad Yunus, creator of microfinance initiatives across the world, writes and speaks about the particular advantages of investing in youth employment and youth enterprise.[9] He is very clear that capital must get into the hands of people who are locked in cycles of poverty if they are to develop the kinds of economic and social structures that will truly serve them and their communities.

The consequence of capital starvation is either that new relationship structures have a hard time forming or that those structures begin to fall apart as their initial growth brings them into contact with a larger, better financed society. Contact with the larger society provokes a kind of competition in values, in loyalties, in access to power, and in finances. But the ethic of competition is not always compatible with the ethic of collaboration, and one often ends up overwhelming the other.

In twenty-first-century America this dynamic of competition almost always takes place through battles for legitimacy in terms of credentials. We know how this works in the world of schools: only a few students will be admitted to the "best" schools and colleges. The same pattern holds in the world of economic development. Poor people in general don't have access to capital. However, there are always indigenous community-based enterprises developing naturally in poor communities, because human beings respond to their circumstances by acting in their own interests. Seeking capital, these enterprises look for sponsorship from the broader society. This puts them into competition with each other for outside funds from philanthropists, universities, government agencies—the nonprofit industrial complex.[10] These sponsors then legitimize the indigenous enterprises they choose to fund, and they delegitimize the rest.

Once a community-based enterprise is legitimized in this way, the credentialing process takes on a life of its own. Leaders are promoted. Their résumés become longer. They find themselves with access to more power, money, and authority. And their power, money, and authority then follow them outside their home community into the larger world, threatening to fragment the initial relationships that gave them strength.

In our work in Baltimore, developing a network grounded in cooperative economics, youth employment, and collaborative knowledge work, we have been able to displace the larger society's system of credentials and legitimation. But we decided first to gather substantial capital from outside the community. This decision should be explained clearly. One way to think about the initial influx of capital into poor communities is as reparations. At the end of the Civil War, the federal government made a commitment, soon broken, to stake forty acres and a mule for each formerly enslaved family. In the twenty-first century the economy is no longer predominantly agricultural, but the long-promised stake is just as necessary now. The twenty-first-century equivalent of forty acres and a mule is capital for education. The problem has been that rather than supplying capital for education directly to poor communities, that capital has been effectively put in trust to be held or deployed by powerful interests already dominant in the larger society. With both good intentions and bad, those interests have instituted structures that preserve and aggravate the caste divisions education is theorized to erase.

The argument for the ubiquitous approach of putting funds for education in trust to already-powerful interests is circular: To educate others, you must already be educated yourself. Control of education can therefore be trusted only to those who already hold credentials from the educational system. ("Credentialed," of course, *means* "trust-worthy.") But the credentialing within the educational system is contrived in such a way that the more advanced the credential, the fewer the number of individuals who are thought capable of achieving it. This system exhibits caste stratification in exactly the same way as the society does generally, and control of educational capital never leaves the hands of the relative few.

We therefore began our effort in Baltimore by confronting the question of who is qualified to be trusted with educational capital. Baltimore had already developed a small but intense network of youth-centered Black-controlled organizations that were pressing powerful institutions to recognize the inauthenticity and ineffectiveness of many paternalistic policies. These youth-centered organizations—and in particular, the Baltimore Algebra Project and Leaders of a Beautiful Struggle—insisted that the issue to debate was not whether oppressed people should have a seat at the table but, rather, who the table belongs to in the first place.[11] If it is young people in poverty we're talking about educating, it's the young people's table.

If it's a poor community that is 98 percent African-ancestored, it's *their* table. The fact that White people's money, capital from outside the community, can be helpful is relevant, but that fact doesn't change whose table it is we're talking about. Funds must be held in trust by the community for itself. Understanding these funds as reparations may help people who are confused by questions of ownership. "If it's the White people's money, shouldn't they control it?" Answer: "It's only the White people's money because they stole the wages of enslaved people and then manipulated legal and social policies to preserve economic advantages from the Civil War till today."

This is not only an inescapable point for economic development. It is also inescapable for a people attempting to help its children grow up into a viable society. Growing up means learning to live in a community that is distinguished by culture-specific roles, modes of exchange and representation, discourses, and beliefs. When millions of children have the experience that their growing up is entrusted to people from a different culture—from a culture foreign to their parents and their neighbors—the children can become confused. This point has been made for at least two centuries by thinkers who today are generally called Black Nationalists. But it is actually—as most Nationalists point out—the common understanding of every culture: enculturation must be entrusted to representatives of the culture in question, not to someone else.

How do we break out of the circular reasoning that refuses to respect practitioners of a culture unless they first earn an ever more elaborate string of academic credentials from the dominant institutions? Our solution is to see how authority or credibility emerge in the context of cooperative, economically productive enterprises that are centered on young people and exchanges of knowledge. What we have observed is what you might expect. People gain authority and credibility who know a lot; initiate new actions; keep promises and do what they say they're going to do; attract resources (financial, social, physical, and so on); solve problems; listen well; bring people together who have common or complementary interests; speak persuasively; represent the collective's ideas and interests in effective ways; and encourage openness.

This is hardly mysterious. Many officials in the larger society have long lists of degrees and credentials but are distrusted because they are unreliable, ignorant, aloof, secretive, or deceitful. Authority is achieved through action in a social context, not necessarily through obtaining a certificate from a dominant institution. I am simply pointing out that authority develops in human societies well before bureaucratic credentialing develops. Credentialing often functions not to identify who actually is authoritative in a given context but rather to restrict access to power and to maintain control over the kinds and castes that will be permitted to make decisions about resources.

Respecting authority as it naturally arises in communities, creating a new legitimacy that rejects inauthentic credentialing structures is far from a novel idea. There are many historical precedents, notably the American Revolution, which challenged the credentialing powers of the King of England; or the prolonged insurgency of enslaved and formerly enslaved persons demanding citizenship rights before and after the Civil War, in effect challenging the credentialing powers of White supremacists. Another important historical example is the Zapatista revolution, which challenged the credentialing structures of neoliberalism and of the global economy. On January 1, 1994, the Zapatistas asserted both their territorial and their cultural integrity, enforced through armed struggle, with the goal of establishing indigenous authority in the Lacandon Jungle of southern Mexico. They determined for themselves that the property structures of the neoliberal world order made no sense for Indigenous people, and they fought to defend their self-determined relationships to the land, to each other, and to the larger world.

These challenges to political and economic authority are always accompanied by parallel changes in educational structures. In the early United States, for example, Noah Webster successfully instituted an entire system of literacy, complete with spellings, pronunciations, definitions, and pedagogies that were accepted by the country as especially suited to the young and historically novel democracy. The Zapatista education and university structures have emerged in forms directly influenced by Paolo Freire's and Ivan

Illich's principles of deschooling combined with Indigenous people's practices. And the African American educational philosophy centers on a consciously Black authority in the midst of White supremacy.

But the dominant society's system of credentials and administration is extremely well entrenched. We are at the tail end of two hundred years of techniques for managing schools "rationally." We are not yet ready in the United States for a Zapatista-style overthrow of dominant structures. Nevertheless, our parallel political economy, powered by peer-to-peer knowledge work, has found crawl spaces in the hollows of the dominant system, and our work is enlarging those spaces. Authoritative leaders emerge through their practice in community. Their authority is not conferred by existing institutions, but in some circumstances existing institutions find themselves supporting these locally authoritative leaders incidentally, when, for example, their abilities fit the structure of requirements for a diploma or lead to a fee-for-service contract or impress in some other way. Our new educational network is being built alongside the old one. It is not directly opposed; it uses some of the same material, even some of the same techniques and funding streams as the oppressive system. But we keep it at arm's length; we are careful not to be wrapped up or dragged into that inextricable knot that makes everything stay more or less as it has been.

Flexible and daring, we use the tools that come to hand and move as opportunities present themselves but always in directions of our own choosing, regardless of what anyone else may think.

PART II

RE-ROOTING EDUCATION

CHAPTER 4

An Educational Bureaucracy Built on Violence

Selections

My wife and I sit with our eighth grader in his school cafeteria, with many other parents and their eighth graders, for the annual introduction to Baltimore's high school admissions process. An official shows slides with "composite scores" for the three or four "selective" high schools—some mysterious computation of weighted test scores, grades, and attendance required for admission. Our son wants to enroll in the high school his older brothers went to, but he will need a minimum composite score, we are told, of 620, whatever that means. Friends pass on the rumor that nothing less than a 680 would guarantee a place. What are our children thinking? Are their stomachs knotting up like ours?

In 2018 only ten Black students in a class of more than eight hundred were admitted to Stuyvesant High School, the selective public school in New York that my father graduated from in 1944, also with exactly ten Black students in his class.[1] Today, the admissions-by-testing high schools in New York are 4 percent Black and Latinx, compared to 70 percent Black and Latinx students in the system's population overall. A recent study commissioned by Baltimore's school system determined that students who grow up in low-income census tracts are much less likely to qualify for the top-rated high schools.[2] Another study of Baltimore City students showed that only 9 percent of students who entered high school in 2002 had earned any post-secondary college degree at all by 2011, either two-year or four-year, and virtually all of that 9 percent had attended one of three selective high schools.[3]

Yet another study from roughly the same period demonstrates that there is an almost nine-year difference in life expectancy for Baltimore residents with low educational opportunity compared to those with high educational opportunity: dying at age sixty-eight rather than at seventy-seven, on average.[4] The adolescents sitting to the left and the right of us in the cafeteria, and our own Black son, are learning about a process of unscientific, arbitrary evaluations that correlate with scientifically well-documented results in terms of life and death, not to mention illness, incarceration, unemployment, and poverty. The children who must take the city bus because their parents can't drive them to school, for example, have worse attendance than their peers—through no fault of their own—and so they have lower composite scores and less access to selective high schools, and they are expected to die almost a decade before their wealthier peers.

The selective high schools all across our country, the division into wealthy suburban and underfunded urban and rural jurisdictions, and the stratification of the country's educational arrangements can hide neither the life-and-death consequences of their selectivity nor the arbitrariness of their process. In the precise location that is now the entrance to Baltimore's baseball stadium, a slave market prospered for decades. Selections were made, prices negotiated, families separated, and human beings sold as property, many for transportation to sugar plantations down South where an early death was almost certain. In certain Israeli towns, "admissions committees" select exclusively Jewish residents by rejecting Palestinian applicants on the basis—written into law—that they are unsuitable to the community's "social characteristics"—the characteristic, especially, of being Jewish.[5] The Italian Jewish writer Primo Levi describes the prayer of one inhabitant of the Auschwitz concentration camp, a certain prisoner named Kuhn, who was spared in the selection for the gas chamber. Levi writes,

> Kuhn is out of his mind. Does he not see, in the bunk next to him, Beppo the Greek, who is twenty years old and is going to the gas chamber the day after tomorrow, and knows it, and

lies there staring at the light without saying anything and without even thinking anymore? . . . Does Kuhn not understand that what happened today is an abomination, which no propitiatory prayer, no pardon, no expiation by the guilty— nothing at all in the power of man to do—can ever heal?

If I were God, I would spit Kuhn's prayer out upon the ground.[6]

Young people in the eighth grade who are left out of selections for top-ranked schools are not, of course, doomed. Far from it. This book hopes to multiply their power for doing good and for living rich lives of struggle and creation. If we who believe in freedom are successful, then there will be many places that establish their own criteria for intellectual and cultural excellence, not beneath or above but parallel to other criteria. But the current structures of education in America cannot hide their roots, cannot hide their effects; we should tell the truth about them, and we should heed those who warn us to beware of tendencies in human nature that have been known to follow a steel logic all the way to an inhuman end.

Schools

It is easy to be fooled. The problem of education in the twenty-first century is that we do encounter young people in schools, and that is where their parents want them to be. Many people agree that schools do great harm, but relatively few conclude that the students should stop going. I have spent my adult life working in schools of poverty, though I think they are often damaging. But I have tried not to let myself be fooled. No matter how many smart people put their minds to the puzzle of the "achievement gap," equality will not be found under the structure of American education as it has evolved from the Civil War to the present day. A culture's system of education helps children grow up into the society they actually live in. Our society is arranged to be unequal in outcomes, and so our system of education helps children learn to cope with inequality, not to undo inequality.

You cannot change a culture's system of education without changing the culture. But we have been fooled into thinking that education reform is possible, separate from cultural reform, because we have accepted the idea that schools are somehow autonomous cultural integers that could be picked up, put down, funded, replicated, populated by interchangeable faculty or students, commodified, traded, purchased, or sold (with profit to be skimmed off the transactions). In fact, schools are not discrete integers; they are threaded into communities, which are themselves threaded or knotted into the country's social, economic, political, and historical arrangements.

When we think of students and schools, the resulting web of relationships is complicated enough in itself. But the young people in schools see themselves as much more than just students in relation to an educational system. They are involved not only in the tasks prescribed by teachers and administrators; they are also members of their families—continuously representing their families or rebelling against their families or trying to evade or maintain their families. They also represent, rebel against, question, or emerge into their own identities as man, woman, neither, or both; into their ethnic and cultural identities; into their identity as "having a boyfriend" or "having a girlfriend" or being unattached; as being employed or musical or "conscious" or religious or political or goofy or into drugs or drinking or skating. What is primary for any person at any moment may be influenced by an institution such as school, but school or any other institution never *determines* what is primary for anyone, ever.

A culture is made up of many strands running through individuals, and it is influenced in small and large ways by those individuals on their own or in groups. "Education" is the name for the natural function of human cultures whereby young people grow up to weave themselves somehow or other into the general fabric. Our culture—twenty-first-century American culture—has evolved into a fabric with grotesque knots and clumps, and our schools of poverty are the places where we expect young people to contort themselves to match these grotesque shapes.

Cultural forces twist and sometimes break young people, trying and failing to force them into the weave of the fabric. They see the problem at very close range, right down at the level of the cloth, and they feel themselves palpably pulled into these ridiculous knotted clumps, fearful from the start that they are going to get stuck there like everyone else. We adults, our perspective lifted up a little higher from the level of the cloth and a little more practiced in our analysis, think we can distinguish the individual threads and strands, and we believe, given more time and maybe some tools, that we could pick open the intricacies of the educational/social/political/economic/racial/gendered mess and smooth a path for some more weaving, to draw more students comfortably into the warp and weft of the fabric. But we have been mistaken again and again. We usually make the knots worse. Our perspectives have fooled us. These knots won't come undone through even the smartest untangling.

Scam

The current educational system in America can best be described as a scam, a fraud, a confidence trick, where someone gets your money, and you get little or nothing in return. The purpose of the scam, the goal behind it, is to maintain the racialized caste structure and property relations of the country as they currently operate. Schools play a leading role in establishing and maintaining the caste structure. Parents confront this role directly through the "choices" they make of where their children will be educated. Each school clearly communicates its position: some are high, some are low, some are positioned as gateways to higher status, and some are positioned as escapes from the dead-end bottom, though they offer only a stoop to sit on while a world with more opportunity marches by. But every school has its place in the hierarchy, and students and families and teachers in every school have a pretty good idea of what that place is. In fact, "Know your place," is the principal lesson schools teach.

But human beings do not easily accept being pushed down. They must be taught to accept oppression. One teaching method is violence. Another teaching method is fraud: a trickster with advanced degrees and qualifications performs research, collects data, compares and contrasts, and then announces that the people on the bottom are correctly placed and that the people on the top—including himself and his children—deserve to be on top and should be compensated accordingly. This trickster is, in effect, every teacher, every principal, every educational bureaucrat, every politician, every voter, to whatever extent we go along with the testing and the grading and the reporting of our assessments that end up consigning students to divergent, inequitable paths.

The scam works. Many people, maybe even most—not only on the top but also on the bottom and in the middle—believe that their position within the social and economic hierarchy is more or less a fair reflection of their ability. Some are bitter about it; some are pleasantly surprised; but most accept that they are as good or bad at learning as their grades and scores say they are. The success of the scam makes it appear natural that the "smart" people should get easier access to "better" colleges, "better" neighborhoods, and higher paying jobs.

This confidence game is an elaborate one that has evolved over centuries. It is deeply entwined with the country's political, economic, and geographic arrangements, and it is all designed to conceal the patently obvious fact that not merit but property determines the larger trajectory of educational outcomes. Our starting point is understanding how the current system is all about sorting. It mirrors the sorting by property into rich and poor, haves and have nots. The sorting that schools do is a physical sorting. It is a literal segregation not justified any longer overtly by race but now by more subtle "scientific" quantifiable abstractions—test scores, assessments. Almost no one complains about the assistance a student might receive from the apparently unimpeachable and "natural" institution of the family. Wealthy children—regardless of their merit—grow up in wealthy families. The children of the poor—regardless of their merit—grow up in poor families. The families of the wealthy buy homes in jurisdictions with the best schools or pay for private schools; the families of the poor make do with whatever inferior schooling is available in neighborhoods they can afford. The families of the rich buy healthy food in sufficient quantities to help their children—meritorious and not—achieve in school, and they take vacations in interesting places to broaden their children's experiences and perspectives. The families of the poor teach their children to cope with an empty fridge and to endure summers with too much idle time and too few safe places to run around. Not merit but property determines the distribution of educational benefits—property possessed and deployed through the institution of the family.

But this fact is bound to another fact, that property is not enjoyed or even defined in the absence of state power. Policing and incarceration—which both threaten and use physical force—are the institutions that protect property. The relationship between the family, property, and state power is concealed by the false idea that merit is rewarded. School is where children "learn" that families with more money earned their status, a piece of knowledge that greatly facilitates deference to inequalities in the distribution of property, reducing the need for the state to exercise direct physical control on the less propertied classes. David Stovall points out that in this system of violence the term "school-to-prison pipeline" can be misleading, because it implies that school is different from prison. The key feature of the continuum on which both institutions exist in the lives of oppressed people is that both are utterly reliant on violence and threats of violence to control the populations confined in them.[7]

The most important educational inequality in the twenty-first century is the geographic segregation of one school district from another. If your parents can afford to live in an expensive jurisdiction, you can go to a fine school. If your parents cannot afford the expensive jurisdiction, you don't *choose* the poorer jurisdiction; you live in it by necessity. And of course, even within jurisdictions, wealthier subgroups live in wealthier neighborhoods and have better schools. Poorer subgroups are compelled to use what's left over.

How is this geographic segregation by wealth enforced? Buy or rent a home in a neighborhood you can't afford, and the bank or landlord will eventually initiate a legal process so that sheriffs or paid agents can physically evict you. The disproportionate effect of the foreclosure crisis on African American families is not only a housing issue; geography also determines the quality of the schools children are zoned to attend. Many of the Black families who disproportionately lost their homes or their jobs because of the 2008–2012 recession also lost access to schools with integrated or predominantly middle-class populations.[8] Foreclosure and eviction are the specific legal mechanisms that segregate populations in both housing *and* education. And geographic segregation is enforced by violence, by the rich compelling the poor physically to put their bodies and their belongings somewhere else and then compelling them to send their children to some other jurisdiction's schools. Even the verbal act of falsely declaring your family's place of residence to be within the boundaries of a better school district constitutes a felony in most jurisdictions, and this crime is sometimes prosecuted.[9] Geographic school segregation is written into law and backed by force, just as patrols are assigned to keep people of color from trespassing on White people's enclaves.

Trayvon Martin's encounter with George Zimmerman in 2012 epitomizes the presumption of guilt that a hoodie can represent to White patrols in certain neighborhoods. Property is threatened by the mere existence of Black people, the patrollers believe. But it is harder for us to see that the same logic is applied to education. In the White imagination, the distribution of supposedly scarce educational opportunities is also threatened by the existence of Black people. No other explanation could possibly be given for the continued and in fact increasing segregation of public schools, two-thirds of a century after *Brown v. Board*. A majority of White people find ways to be sure that their children are safe from the educational threat of Black children, and this task can only be accomplished through actual physical separation——through moving to another neighborhood or jurisdiction, through driving their children to different schools, through paying for a private education that most Black families cannot afford because of the country's history of White rapacity. The epicenter of Baltimore's 2015 Uprising, Frederick Douglass High School——named after one of America's greatest heroes and the alma mater of Thurgood Marshall, strategist and tactician behind

Brown v. Board's complex challenge to de jure segregation—has not a single White student enrolled. It is listed in the state's statistics as 100 percent Black.

The education system depends on violence and threats of violence exactly as much as the larger society does. "Ability" tracking requires that adolescent bodies be in a specific place at a specific time, because of their test scores. Students are assigned to follow directions corresponding to the grades and test scores that sort them with others who have putatively similar profiles. First comes the tracking into "selective" versus "nonselective" schools. With great cruelty, we pretend that young children deserve or don't deserve to be in places of opportunity based on absurd evaluations. We teach children and families to accept grades on report cards and scores on tests as wages of talent and effort, though we know that socioeconomic status predicts academic achievement more closely than any other factor. Then, as children grow up, we teach them to cash in their report cards and test scores at each new barrier in order to gain admission to the next segregated environment—segregated in the sense that the other children, with worse grades, will be kept out.

If those excluded students don't want to be in the precise room to which they have been tracked at the precise time they are scheduled to be there, they will count as truant or "hall walkers" or "cutters." If they stay away from the school building altogether, they may be picked up by specially designated, often armed truancy patrols and forcibly brought to school. What happens to hall walkers? In the more orderly schools, they are "swept" from floor to floor (from the Vietnam War–era military tactic "sweep and clear") until they arrive at a specified location where they will be compelled to remain until an arbitrarily determined dismissal releases them—another physical confinement.

And if they refuse this further in-school physical confinement, they will be sent home. That is, they will be ordered out of the building and physically prevented from entering again until they have accepted that the school has the authority to position all students' bodies where and when it chooses, using any criteria it sees fit provided those criteria include references to grades, test scores, and behavioral records, not explicitly to the underlying criteria of race and wealth.

And if the student still refuses to leave the school and go home, then the authorities have no other choice but to have security or police lock the poor child up. Wealthier and Whiter families generally do not have to witness such violence in their own schools and communities. But from my first year teaching in Baltimore, 1987, until the present in the jail where I teach, I have watched again and again and again (as most Baltimore City schoolchildren and teachers have watched) while a security guard or police officer removes a young person from a classroom or hallway because they refuse to leave a space where they are not permitted. In schools as in jail, such action is perfectly normal, unremarkable. Physical control is an indispensable expectation in schools of poverty. The excuse, of course, is that the young person is or was "disruptive" in some way: "They must be segregated because they are disruptive." No. They are disruptive because they have been segregated.

Tracking is enforced through violence. As in most societies, state-approved violence is refined through the mechanism of the scapegoat. Not everyone needs to be kept in place by force; it is sufficient to humiliate, torture, exclude, or exile a few or a group, piling symbolic transgressions on their heads so that a whole class of human beings will be kept down, or so that the lust for vengeance can be confined to a relatively small field of play. Our current system of education does this by making examples of the students who rebel, ensuring that their grades and rankings consign them to futures no one would willingly choose. It is much simpler if students just accept where they are placed according to their identified merit, which means, on average, according to the caste status of their family. The universal view is that once they learn the lessons of school, they will defer without a fuss.

This system of lies, unworthy of a free people, benefits those classes that have already accumulated a great deal of material wealth. It preserves the economic and political advantages that institutional racism gives to White people, who benefited and continue to benefit from the uncompensated or undercompensated labor of Black people and other people of color over centuries. And this fraud is now advanced in such a way that even more profit is extracted through the deals that private entities are making with public school systems. This economic arrangement becomes more and more important as the economy shifts from industrial production to knowledge work. All around the world the education industry is funneling public money to private accumulations. Testing, training, curriculum, professional development, technology, and many layers of monitoring and control are multibillion-dollar private industries that provide little benefit to poor children.

Many young people in poverty feel in their bodies how wrong all this is and have their own analyses of causes and effects. They tend to resist. They cause considerable turbulence in what the authorities wish were smoother, less contentious operations. But the authorities have a strategy of their own to neutralize young people's defiant acts: the idea of merit. "You may ignore our policies and disrupt our plans," they say, "but we will withhold grades and diplomas and exclude you from our property, by force if necessary. If you merit inclusion, you may come in and accept the ranking we offer."

The owning classes will not willingly abandon the misguided logic of meritocracy. The widespread insurgency of the 1960s compelled certain institutions to allow some people of color and many women into the ranks of power and property, but the ideology of merit was left intact: schools still teach everyone, rich and poor, that the way out of poverty is through talent and hard work. Without this dogma, what remains is simply the obvious injustice. But the logic of meritocracy teaches that your status is your own fault, dulling the impulse to rise up, and diverting energy toward the channels approved by the powerful.

The uprisings in Ferguson, Oakland, Chicago, Baltimore, and elsewhere prove the rule. Although oppressed people often endure suffering without causing much trouble, between 2014 and 2016 thousands of people blocked traffic, shut down cities, and made themselves heard. But these uprisings were not a response to the injustice perpetrated in schools; they were triggered by judicially sanctioned police violence. Although the education system may scam us into thinking our social status is our own fault, people draw the line at being murdered by the police—as if being alive were a property to which everyone is entitled unconditionally. "Merit" shouldn't determine whether police shoot you. The right to life, at least, seems to be independent of "talent" and "hard work," and therefore violations of this basic human right led to resistance.[10]

Young people rose up, and the owning classes defended themselves through official—as opposed to rogue—state violence. In Baltimore, for example, students marched, and some destroyed property. Police responded with riot shields, tear gas, and clubs, and then the governor ordered the state's militia and tanks to occupy the city. The message was clear: Black lives are not valued as much as the owning classes' property.

In the wake of police violence, students marched to protect their lives. But students do not march or destroy property in the United States to protect their education. They do not rise up, for example, when they are assigned to a classroom that can only find a long-term substitute because of the shortage of teachers, or when they are refused admission to selective high schools, or when their registration at college is canceled because their grades were low, or they simply could not afford tuition. Advancement through the educational system is not a right in America. It is thought to be earned. This idea is generally accepted by rich and by poor. Therefore, blame for failing to advance does not fall on the powerful; it falls on the young people themselves and on their families.

Instead of teaching that the sorting of human beings by property necessitates the violence of police and school control, our system of education teaches that each student's individual merit necessitates the sorting. I am expected to defer to my classification. There will be physical consequences if I don't; I will either be coerced to remain in an ever more segregated space, or some official authority will actually put their hands on me. There are other kids, the good kids, who get classified differently. They are expected to defer as well.

It is this attitude of deference that is crippling and destructive. We understand that to defer to violence—though often, to preserve our lives, we must—is outrageous and humiliating. Black Lives

Matter is a collective response to this outrage: we will defer no more. Claude McKay wrote,

> If we must die, let it not be like hogs
> Hunted and penned in an inglorious spot,
> While round us bark the mad and hungry dogs.[11]

This was the nondeferential, nonconforming attitude of Black veterans returning from the World Wars to the South and responding to the "persuasion" of White violence by taking up arms, undergirding and protecting the civil rights and Black Power movements: sometimes nonviolent, sometimes not; in places following charismatic leaders, in places digging deep into patient grassroots organizing, but everywhere enacted by people who could not be cowed.[12]

But *Brown v. Board* and the significant successes of the movement initiated a specious argument that the American education system has run with ever since: "Now that segregation and discrimination have ended, the only thing holding back Black people is themselves. Hard work and merit will be rewarded. You can be anything you want to be. Nothing stands in your way." This post-*Brown* creed is poison, because it has taught, or tried to teach, four or five generations to defer to the false meritocratic sorting by tests and grades and attendance data. Although human beings see direct physical intimidation as an insult and affront to our dignity, the evaluation of our worth through these school measurements of merit is confusing; we often turn our sense of insult and affront back on ourselves as shame.

This is indeed the post-*Brown* creed now taught by school, but it has only been taught imperfectly. It doesn't sit well. I think it is vital for everyone who believes in freedom to remind young people that they do not need to defer to the judgments of the schools and the sorting. It is even heroic to stand up to those judgments. It is as heroic to stand up to those judgments as it is to stand up to more obvious threats of violence against you, against your friends, against your family, against your race.

How do we help young people do this?

An Organizing Question

"How do we help students stand up to the sorting and violence?" is an organizing question; we are trying to protect space so that young people can do something for themselves. The immediate task is *not* to stop the sorting *for* them. The immediate task is to support their refusal to defer. This is a question about how to create structures, relationships, knowledge, language, and power that will organize the resistance of young people to the violence of schools in ways that let them emerge into a living future.[13]

The difference between trying to fix the problem for them and helping them to organize is crucial. We can think about this difference in historical terms. In the middle of the youth insurgency of the 1960s, the problem of educational sorting was thoroughly analyzed. Advocates identified busing and open admissions as policies that could undo the effects of racial or ability-based segregation. Forced busing took students of one ethnicity out of their neighborhood and into the neighborhood of another ethnicity in an attempt to create desegregated schools. Open admissions relaxed or completely eliminated entrance requirements in formerly selective programs, schools, and colleges in an attempt to desegregate access to high-status institutions. These policies generated bitter controversy, consumed billions of dollars in resources, and didn't work to change the structure of race and class power. As the dominant society shifted its racial discourse to allow "qualified" individuals access to high-status roles regardless of ethnicity, consensus in the African American community about the pernicious effects of educational sorting fell apart. A new Black bourgeoisie felt that its own children could get access to the spoils of the dominant society without having to change the structure of that society.[14] Busing and open admissions no longer made sense to them, and it had never made sense to most White families. In the new less discriminatory world, those policies would only open up access for students seen as unqualified or for families who were too dysfunctional, as the bourgeoisie saw it, to get out of the ghetto on their own. Unqualified students or dysfunctional families lacked merit.

Busing and open admissions were not organizing strategies. They did not help the people directly affected by caste oppression learn how to resist oppressive structures. They simply forced open some doors while deferring to the underlying principles of meritocracy and qualification. We are looking for an organizing strategy that is much less deferential to the dominant culture—a strategy that will allow young people to devise for themselves an alternative to ability grouping, winners and losers, the fragmenting of communities, and the institutions of violence. We believe we know what one such strategy looks like.

Noncorporate community-based charter schools, homeschooling, and radical independent schools—especially African-centered or consciously anticolonial ones—have been the best ways out of the current morass for hundreds of thousands of families. Over time, these approaches may have systemic effects. But corporate interests are wide awake and working hard to maintain their institutional advantages. They have, of course, the whole political and economic weight of the country behind them. We who believe in freedom would do well to organize ourselves behind a concrete educational agenda that does more than resist corporatist reforms. Saving public education from the neoliberal attack is saving something that fails to correct the status quo of oppression. Our task is rather to *create* a public education that is worth living and dying for.

That system must be built from the bottom up. That means we must create a political economy of education from the bottom up: youth-centered, youth-staffed mini-societies that have relatively healthy patterns of human relationships but also mini-societies that have relatively stable economic footing thoughtfully networked together in politically powerful ways. These mini-societies must be spread over relatively extended geographical areas: a few neighborhoods in a city, a few cities, some Indigenous lands, or a rural county or two. The parallel system does not need to replace the establishment educational system right away, though eventually we intend that it will.

The Paradox of Command

The political and educational strategy of youth enterprises described in this book focuses on enacting our learning from below, conceiving the periphery as central. Whenever we push the superintendent or mayor to change policies, curriculum, or funding priorities (as we *must* push them), we are likely to slip into thinking that someone at the top of the educational structure might "solve" our educational problems. They cannot. Education is only the expression of a culture. We create our own culture from our daily acts, or else we defer to someone else's culture imposed from outside.

I have been emphasizing the youth enterprises as locations of egalitarian collective practices in contrast to the classrooms, schools, and districts of today, which are emphatically authoritarian and unjust. You cannot learn to live in a democracy by attending most twenty-first-century American schools. You can only learn your place in a caste-determined structure. But it is nevertheless easy to be fooled into thinking that the right mayor or CEO or school board or governor could establish and implement policies that would create humane schools for everyone. This is incorrect. The chiefs are relatively powerless—responding to the received culture, much more than creating it. In fact, their position as pretend deciders of our actions tends to impede initiative and coordinated action at the grassroots level.

How do we understand the incapacity of the CEOs, the mayors, the school principals, and the boards of education? I find Leo Tolstoy's *War and Peace* helpful in analyzing this problem. *War and Peace* describes the tragedy that results from commanders' ignorance of the difference between what they say should happen on the battlefield and what actually happens. The end of the novel is an extended study of this state of affairs in the context of Napoleon's 1812 invasion of Russia and his eventual retreat:

> For a command to be executed with certainty it is necessary that a man should command what can be executed. But to know what can and what cannot be executed is impossible, not only in the case of Napoleon's campaign in Russia, in

which millions participated, but even in the most uncomplicated event, for in either case millions of obstacles may arise to prevent its execution. Every command executed is always one of an immense number unexecuted.[15]

In light of Tolstoy's observation, it is probably best to consider with a good sense of humor the fifty or one hundred or two hundred years (depending how you want to count) of education reform in the United States.[16] How many of the commands given by thousands of superintendents have been executed as intended? How many reforms have succeeded? Some certainly. But the great majority have not. The important point, however, is not the small proportion of successful to unsuccessful commands; the important point is that authorities believe they are commanding at all—making things happen—when in fact the relation of command to action "on the ground" is much more interdependent and subtle.

"A military organization," Tolstoy writes, "may be quite accurately compared to the figure of a cone, the base of which, with the largest diameter, consists of the rank and file; the next higher and smaller section of the cone consists of the next higher grades of the army, and so on to the apex, the point of which will represent the commander in chief."[17] This structure applies, as Tolstoy points out, to "every sort of administration," including the American school with teachers at the base, department heads and principals—higher and smaller in number—central office people, and superintendents (or with students at the base of the cone if you prefer to see students as the most subordinate rank in one army of common purpose, rather than as the enemy, or, less bellicosely, the "client").

Tolstoy continues,

The soldiers, of whom there are the greatest number, form the lower section of the cone and its base. The soldier himself does the stabbing, hacking, burning, and pillaging and always receives orders for these actions from people above him; he himself never gives an order. The noncommissioned officer (of whom there are fewer) performs the action itself [for example, stabbing and shooting] less often than the soldier, but he gives a certain number of commands. An officer still less often acts directly himself, and still more frequently commands. A general does nothing but command the army and hardly ever uses a weapon himself. The commander in chief never takes direct part in the action but only gives general orders concerning the movements of the mass of troops.

Tolstoy sees this phenomenon as

> a law by which men, to take common action, combine in such relations that the more directly they participate in the action the more numerous they are and the less they command, while the less direct their participation in the action, the fewer they are and the more they command, rising in this way from the lowest ranks to the man at the top, who takes the very least direct share in the action and, more than all the rest, devotes his activity to commanding.[18]

The distance between the rank-and-file and their commanders is seen here as a difference between action and speech.

If the superintendent issues a directive and the effect intended by the directive is not achieved, does it still make sense to say, "The superintendent mandated/directed such and such?" Tolstoy would argue that it does not make sense. He describes what we might call a command as actually just the arbitrary relationship between some words from on high and some actions down below. Many empty commands are given, meaning they are never reflected in what is actually happening on the battlefield; only a few of what Tolstoy would define as genuine commands correspond to what the lower ranks are actually doing. Commanders insist in those few cases, however, that power was exercised to achieve a particular result, but Tolstoy describes a much subtler relationship between command and power. Genuine commands, in Tolstoy's view, are only apparent in retrospect. They are less like orders and more like good guesses about what is possible and what might happen in the field. If an order does not match what actually happens in the field, it is not, according to Tolstoy, a command at all.

The data-driven regime in education is an excellent contemporary example of the phenomenon Tolstoy describes. The state superintendent and the district superintendents issue directives for tests to be given and for students to care about them and for teachers to implement curriculum faithfully in ways that alter the brain states of children such that they select the right answers on the tests. These administrators further direct that students move to the next grade or do not and that teachers are given raises, are punished, or are fired based on their success or failure in having adjusted so many brain states in such and such ways.

But the Russian winter and the fear and hunger of his soldiers and the stubbornness of the enemy resulted in such a vast number of Napoleon's commands evaporating with no relationship to the actions of actual human beings that the French armies retreated back to France exhausted and decimated even after Napoleon declared they had "won" the battle for Moscow. And the implementation of massive testing regimens, despite the commands of Harvard-trained superintendents and CEOs, falls to pieces, bears no methodical relationship to the millions of actions of teachers and students, actions that manifestly do not result in the correct answers being selected on the standardized tests.

Only the students are fully aware that no command has actually been given unless there is a correspondence between the words of the superior and the actions of the subordinate. So they boycott the tests, or walk out of school, or click random answers, or try to answer a few questions and then quit, or simply stay in bed, not bothering to come to school for these useless tests at all.

Tolstoy is also explicit about the social function of the mistaken idea that the commanders at the top of the pyramid control the actions of those at the bottom:

> Those who do not take direct part in the action [the superintendents and administrators] devise considerations, justifications and conjectures concerning their collective activity. . . . Such justifications release those who cause the events from moral responsibility. These temporary aims

[the considerations and justifications] are like the brooms attached to the front of locomotives to clear the snow from the rails: they clear man's moral responsibility from his path. Without these justifications, there could be no solution to the very simplest question that presents itself when examining each historical event. How is it that millions of men commit collective crimes—war, murders, and so on?

Collective crimes in the context of public education are the daily humiliations students endure in schools that manifestly do little good, that lift far too few from poverty, and that preserve a caste system in which the poor die young. The failure of the American system of education, not just for poor children but for all castes, allows Americans to bomb, invade, starve, and exploit millions of people all across the globe, while we exhaust the earth's natural wealth. How is it that people commit these collective crimes? They commit them under color of the considerations, justifications, and conjectures supplied by the people at the top of the pyramid who mostly talk and command. That talk, those mandates clear the moral responsibility for our actions from our path. We pretend to implement the curriculum, we falsely document how we follow the procedures, we administer the tests because they are mandated, not because we believe they will do much good. Educational "science" says that to teach we must measure, or we won't know what has been learned, and this conclusion results in an emphasis on measurement that constricts and falsifies what we teach and that substitutes rewards and punishments as motivation for the wonder, curiosity, sociability, and desire to learn that almost every child naturally exhibits from birth.

The students who rebel, paradoxically, are the ones who actually accept moral responsibility for their actions. They do not mindlessly comply because someone in authority told them what to do with bizarre, obviously illogical justifications. They choose not to defer. They stand up and dare the consequences. At all levels of the chain of command, we must figure out how to get on the same page with those rebels.

I have described the attempt of authorities to compel certain concrete acts from teachers and students. It really cannot be done. No superintendent or administrator, however strong, can "make things happen in schools." The teachers and the students are the actors, and they never cede their authority to act in their own interests. Successful administrators and successful teachers understand what people at the bottom are already doing for their own purposes, and they shape directives that emphasize certain elements in how the people are already moving. Real effects are only possible when supportive pulling from above meets pushing from below. Administrators can effectively encourage, open possibilities, direct funding, and deepen reflection. But this support must follow the actions of the people; authorities cannot compel obedience.

Not only do the justifications of school administrators clear moral responsibility from our path, they also grease the wheels for billions of dollars' worth of business. First, there is the personal business of employment. Teachers, support staff, and lower-level administrators get and keep their jobs in the system because they parrot the considerations, justifications, and conjectures that are in fashion. The historian Thomas Kuhn shows conclusively how the dominant paradigm in science determines which research programs will be funded.[19] And the dominant paradigm in other sectors—in this case education—similarly determines the discourse and habits of those who will be successful in seeking and keeping employment. There are also billions of dollars' worth of interests in the state and federal education apparatus, billions more in colleges and universities, and billions more in private industry—both for-profit and nonprofit: research, testing materials, curriculum, hardware, software, professional associations, and increasingly even instruction both in private charters and in online courses.

On one side of the education coin is the naked economic interest of those who work in the field. But on the other side of the coin is the broader social mandate (however disingenuous) to "educate all children" through efficient administration by directive and command. No one wants to argue for *inefficiency*; but by swallowing the argument for efficient administration, we find ourselves swallowing the related economic interests as well.

We will be stuck in this rut as long as we continue to believe in the usefulness of the bureaucratic pyramid. If we think that skilled superintendents and administrators can run efficient school systems in which teachers faithfully implement curriculum and students are motivated to do their homework, we will continue to founder in a sea of inequality. The colleges and universities and think tanks and journals will continue to produce quasi-scientific justifications for more data and stricter protocols, and the engine of capitalist commerce will continue to monetize these justifications, ensuring continued extraction of billions of dollars from public coffers and from the pockets of the poor.

People at the top of the pyramid talk; people at the bottom of the pyramid do; and the whole pyramid is designed with all kinds of clever channels and gutters to direct the rainfall of public funding into reservoirs of wealth for the already wealthy. Very little of the water poured over this structure ends up turning the mill wheels of education, because it is the wrong structure. The administrative pyramid will never meet the educational needs of a democratic people.

Diffuse Power versus Centralized Power

Fostering the development of youth enterprises and finding ways for them to support each other in networks or federations will have much greater educational impact than the directives of superintendents and school boards. A very few superintendents or other high officials who truly want change will eventually be helpful. But they will follow us. We ourselves need to follow positive energy wherever we find it on the bottom and at the margins of the hierarchy.

Centralized power is inefficient if our goal is to amplify the acts of young people on the periphery. Our strategy is, instead, to diversify the location of decisions, spreading out the power to determine resource allocation, procedures, norms, methods, assignments, and purposes across all the neighborhoods that young people come from. Schools as institutions currently revolve too tightly in the gravitational field of our inequitable caste system to be useful in distributing power more broadly. Community-based youth enterprises are much better suited to this task, as I hope this book is making clear.

These are not new ideas, but they are ideas that have always been at war with another set of ideas. Some scholars might look to Freire, Illich, or Dewey, representatives of a line of thinking that conceives of learning as emerging from cooperative engagement in shared purposes. They look for authoritative teaching not in a priestly caste but in the common people's collaborative efforts to correct human and natural relationships. This strategy, however, goes much further back than Freire, Illich, and Dewey. Their twentieth-century description puts in educational terms what has traditionally been fought over in political, economic, and especially religious contexts. This modern shift makes sense, because the underlying mechanisms of economic production have moved from agricultural to industrial to computational forms of organization. Education is now at the center of all large cultural struggles because production has become so dependent on symbolically encoded information. But the form of the struggle is essentially unchanged: We can understand that knowledge, power, and the nature of relationships are determined by a few people with privileged access to eternal truths. Or we can understand that shared experience constantly generates new combinations of knowledge, power, and relationship among the common people for common purposes, and we can weave a cultural fabric that does not rely on any particular person's ego, though it includes many particular persons.

Advocating for one belief system or the other is not simply a "choice" that a teacher, student, parent, or other citizen makes. It is not a question about weighing up the evidence for one point of view or the other and then taking action. The setting for liberatory education is not a laboratory. It is much more like a theater, and so we should not expect clean, uncontaminated data. The actions of one character lead immediately to the reactions of another. And the meaning of the action cannot be restricted to the meaning of one character's choices and emotions but must be understood as something much larger and more difficult to contain.

It is important for someone enacting a Freirean approach to education, for example, not to defer to an arbitrary authority. But any refusal to defer, in the context of a technocratic educational system, results in a crackdown and, ultimately, as we have seen, in violence or threats of violence. When we refuse to defer, we have already experienced that violence or at least threats of violence in the past, and we can foresee them in the future. And therefore part of the meaning of our action—if we still refuse to defer—is a kind of obstinacy or courage or stance of defiance which may serve varied purposes: to encourage others; to encourage ourselves; to bear witness; to inform authority that we do not belong to them; to inflict actual harm; to win a little breathing room; to provoke (often in the hope of exposing vulnerability); to distract or mislead; and sometimes, in the extreme, to control the circumstances of one's own failure. In the same way, the meaning of authority's reactions to our acts of non-deference also varies with the context of the larger drama, with the setting, with the sequence of what has come before or will come after, with the character and intelligence of the oppressor, or with the means they have at their disposal.

The new political economy of peer-to-peer enterprises is designed to occupy important pieces of terrain on this ancient stage or battlefield—somewhere suitable for more extensive fortifications. We now require structures complex enough that young people can actually experience growing up in them, where they can come to maturity with sufficiently developed roles that they still find meaningful and materially sustaining work *within* the structure, at the far side of what we usually think of as adolescence.

The question is how to situate the refusal to defer as a *positive* act in a parallel communal context—in our more extensive fortifications. The individual's resistance can have many meanings. Established authority will exert its violence in response. We are evolving organized collective resistance that enacts a partially independent theater, not completely divorced from existing schools but independent enough to generate autonomous power. A young person learns a skill. Through their peer-to-peer enterprise, they share this skill with other young people in their own community, and they earn decent money because of their contribution. Within their enterprise they participate in a process to organize their individual and collective work: shifts, compensation, accountability, programming, content. This organizing work is explicitly democratic and partici-patory—that is, the people most affected are central to the decisions made. But there are older generations present too. There are both slightly older young people, and twenty-to-thirty-year-old adults who have more experience, earn more money, and make sure that the young people are supported in being successful. They teach and guide without denying the young people's power to make decisions for themselves. This is delicate work. They protect against exter-nal threats and also nurture and challenge the adolescent workers within the structure of the youth enterprises. It is the example of the slightly older young people that teaches impressionable adolescents how refusal to defer to the larger society functions as an earned au-thority within the structure of their insurgent fortifications.

And there are elders, veterans of the historical freedom struggle, whose role is to encourage, protect, admonish, and watch. Younger people do. Older people have seen. We recognize the patterns in experience, because we have seen them before, and although each generation must learn to recognize the patterns for themselves, we elders suggest looking in this direction or that direction as the weather shifts, or we stand as a break against forces that may still be too great for the growing institutions to withstand.

CHAPTER 5

Base Communities

Re-rooting Education

Base Communities

A network of autonomous grassroots youth enterprises creates an organizing base for a student insurgency in schools of poverty. When students' roles change, their relationships to each other, to the larger society, and to the individual self must also change. Instead of deference to the long-established but debilitating routines of schooling, grading, testing, and coercive control, young people in peer-to-peer enterprises undertake to construct and adapt new forms of being that may satisfy their needs and desires.

We know that these changes take place wherever young people are empowered.[1] But "empowered" does not mean patronized. Empowered does not refer to a forum or an event where young people are allowed to speak within certain adult-controlled parameters but then are ignored or dismissed as inexperienced or unrealistic. In our more precise formula, young people are only empowered when they are doing something adults don't want them to do but find support anyway. If the weaker party's decisions are only affirmed when those decisions coincide with the stronger party's preferences, we are witnessing tokenism, not empowerment. It is only when the people to be empowered actually get their way *despite the objections of the existing power* that a shift has taken place.

This is a difficult standard to meet. In existing schools, if students decide to resist testing, for example, or demand protection from unwarranted search and seizure, adults who want to empower young people should support them. But adults supporting young people against the system's control risk disciplinary actions themselves. I was forced out of a school, for example, when students boycotted state testing, and I supported them. The accepted or safe teacher response when students approach them with an issue like the uselessness of testing is to steer young people away from direct confrontation with school authority. This response usually ends up obstructing the students whose voices we ask to hear. Instead, I referred students to professors at colleges of education, to news articles, and to national coalitions of anti-testing activists—perfectly acceptable teaching practices from the point of view of the construction of knowledge. Supporting students and supporting school administrations are sometimes incompatible activities, because their interests are different. I am only pointing out that we should be truthful about this fact. The interests of teachers and administrators also diverge. No pronouncements from people higher in the chain of command about wanting to empower teachers can be taken seriously until the principals and CEOs are willing to support teachers who reject inhumane mandates and directives.

But these conditions of hypocrisy and coercion are not the end of the story. They are prevalent and insidious, but they are exactly the things we have already decided to struggle against. We are proposing a specific location in poor communities for teaching young people and adults that they *can* struggle: the parallel political economy of peer-to-peer youth enterprises.[2] One outstanding description of this strategy appears in Harold McDougall's *Black Baltimore*,[3] a study from the 1990s of the Sandtown community that was to erupt in 2015, after the death of Freddie Gray.[4] McDougall describes a theory of "base communities" that are needed to support the development of "vernacular culture." He points out that "the civil rights movement severed the bond between the upwardly mobile black middle class, in search of a more universal middle-class status and suburban life, and the black vernacular culture." This left "the great majority of working-class and poor black residents [of Baltimore] . . . consumers of, rather than participants in, the process of political empowerment."[5]

McDougall recommends as a counter-force something he calls "base communities": "small, intimate peer groups of a dozen or two dozen people, in which they can evaluate the day's struggles, commiserate with one another's failures, celebrate success, and plan for the next day's fight. Citizens involved in public debate must also have a safe harbor in which they can try out their opinions and receive succor and support for bruising public combat . . . Families are not large or diverse enough. Churches are too large. The contact must take place in a new, smaller form of association." A network of base communities, McDougall writes, "self-consciously avoids the parochialism and narrow-mindedness we often associate with the old ways, chiefly by resort to the tolerance and vision that are the most positive legacy of the civil rights movement."[6]

Bob Moses, a key leader in the Mississippi theater of the civil rights movement, speaks often of the central function played by meetings as places where ordinary people learn to see themselves as public figures—not in the sense of standing at the front of a room, holding forth or running for office, but in the sense of acting in a public space. They see themselves participating in a public context that has been constituted more formally than a family but not by someone else's formalizations—constituted, rather, by their own meeting's consensus about acceptable structure and procedure. Today, in his capacity as founder of the Algebra Project, Bob Moses says that it is math classrooms where young people must learn to constitute their own public and where they must learn to take over the function of education for themselves as producers of mathematical literacy and other literacies. These classrooms are what McDougall has in mind when he describes base communities. They are not places that reproduce the existing class structure; they are places where students can "fashion an insurgency," as Moses puts it.[7]

The creation of a parallel network or ecosystem of community-based, geographically rooted peer-to-peer youth enterprises is an organizing strategy. It extends McDougall's concept of base community or Bob Moses's concept of the student-facilitated math classroom as meeting space. These are all vernacular cultures that develop their own analyses and agendas, and implement, reflect on, organize, and mature a culture-extending practice rooted in local historical conditions.

Base communities clearly need to stay at arm's length from public bureaucracies, but the development of these enterprises as private entities may be controversial. There is nothing to prevent public school systems from creating their own peer-to-peer employment or governance structures within existing public school frameworks. And it would be useful from an organizing and political point of view for adventurous school administrators and teachers to try to make this happen. The network of Big Picture Schools—which are committed to real-world internships—and African–centered charter schools may be promising vehicles for this kind of public school development. But there is also a need for developing community-based enterprises operating completely independently of government systems.

The existence of the base community does not fit the structure of administrative pyramids and should not be constrained by purposes that are extraneous to the purposes of the participants. McDougall explains that the antidote to the potential parochialism of these autonomous entities is a networking structure—a kind of federalism that will require the shared understanding and joint articulation of priorities and practices. Many radical education and community-based networks already exist or are coming into existence, and "federations" of peer-to-peer enterprises can be thought of on both local and larger scales. To grow the required power, a set of shared principles and a common agenda must eventually be articulated. Somehow or other, parallel institution-building is required to initiate systemic change.

A Community Protects Itself

An anecdote can help illustrate the strategic power of the peer-to-peer enterprises that already form base communities. State violence against Freddie Gray provoked the 2015 Baltimore Uprising of thousands of citizens demanding justice. Marches and rallies organized by young people—many with Algebra Project experience—created a widespread awareness among young people in Baltimore that they could be heard and seen if they acted en masse. When the economy of the city began to be threatened by the numbers of people on the streets, Governor Larry Hogan imposed a curfew, enforced by a military occupation, complete with armored vehicles and National Guard troops. The attorney general of the United States, Lorretta Lynch, visited Baltimore during this occupation and chose the joint offices of Leaders of a Beautiful Struggle and the Baltimore Algebra Project as one of her first stops. Her staff had discovered that these enterprises were populated by organized young people with credibility on the street.

Hundreds of thousands of dollars in contributions to the protest movement poured in from around the country. The most authentic groups structured to receive these funds were coalitions of the same Black-led peer-to-peer enterprises described in this book. As a result, some very young people ended up being the signatories on coalition-controlled bank accounts. Several months later a controversy arose. Suspicions surfaced that some of the funds had not been properly disbursed. The young signatories were suspected of violating financial protocols previously agreed on by the collective. An individual was seen to be profiting at the expense of the community.

In fact, two separate but related problems arose. One question was whether those entrusted with official control of the funds were honest or not. The other question was whether people not directly in control of the funds but who were associated with the grassroots organizations in question could maintain credibility in oppressed communities. "What happened to all that money that came in?" is a question that needs a concrete answer beyond pointing at someone and saying, "I think he stole it."

These are not unusual problems where large amounts of cash are involved in a public project. But the typical solutions often lead to power plays and bitterness, audits, lawyers, forced resignations, and even police and courts. The young people involved could have gone down one of these routes and indeed talked about them. But with support from some older advisors, they decided to use a restorative justice practice instead. Several meetings were convened that brought together the various parties, accusers and accused. Skilled mediators were invited to negotiate an agreement. The parents of some of the young people were also invited to participate, as were community elders. Eventually an agreement between the parties was reached. The agreement included restitution of some portion of the disputed funds on a manageable and generous payment schedule, commitments to maintain college enrollment for one student who it was agreed had gone off track by spending too much time leading demonstrations, and a process for resolving disputes about the conditions of the agreement by conferring with trusted community members if problems surfaced later.

This anecdote shows how culture accrues strength when trust is located at a networked community level. The circumstances could not have been more intense. The whole world was watching Baltimore. Young people were trusted with substantial sums of money, but they were not random young people randomly trusted. They belonged to a coalition of organizations that had earned credibility in the community over the course of years, organizations that were positioned to do some serious work during the high-profile unfolding of Baltimore's story. Some of the young activists found themselves knocked off balance by the intensity of their own need and of the community's need, all swirling together in dramatic currents. But they were not in a rootless community. To the contrary, they were situated among strongly rooted individuals and organizations with many layers of institutional and personal connection, love, and skills. These individuals and organizations were trusted to come together, were authoritative enough to implement and guarantee a solution to a difficult problem, and were able to stabilize the young people involved. The lawyers, police, and courts representing the outside dominant system were kept at bay. A parallel restorative system was deployed using the existing base communities as repositories of cultural strength.

I use this example because the internal conflict was potentially explosive. It illustrates the capacity of networked base communities to cope with real danger. McDougall is particularly good at describing how the language of rights and rights-based organizing can "[isolate] individuals not only from abuses of state power but also from one another, damaging the human networks that were the positive side of the old, vernacular community."[8] The idea that the police and courts should be used to protect the equal rights of all communities certainly makes sense, given existing property relations. But appealing to the police to solve a problem in the Black community, for example, frequently "damages human networks," to put it mildly. This analysis is all too well understood today, when calling the police puts Black life at risk.

Similarly, the idea that public schools should protect the equal right to an education for all communities makes sense. But when a community expects that the vast state-controlled pyramid of educational power will honor the right to an education for all children in the country, human networks are damaged. *Brown v. Board* guaranteed equal educational rights under the law; nevertheless, it resulted in the decimation of whole cadres of Black teachers—teachers who used to be deeply entrenched in poor communities and are no more. In fact, *Brown v. Board* ended up promoting the seductive idea that education is something a community can consume as opposed to being something that communities must produce.

Educational rights, public safety, a viable economics, a viable democracy must be built from the bottom up. Families are vital but too small. It is at the slightly larger scale of the base community or the grassroots enterprise where formal practices enacting rights must be reconceived. Demands for accountability cannot issue from the top of a deracinated pyramid: "the mayor or the governor or the board or the superintendent *mandates.*" Demands for accountability must be made first to ourselves and to our peers, and then, later, from "below" to "above." This was the local strength of the restorative circle that fixed the potentially explosive misappropriation of funds: peers made demands on each other in the context of a relatively healthy and well-rooted network of base communities.

Ubuntu and Place

The beliefs that underlie the new parallel education system we hope to build are less individualistic than they are collective. Instead of being grounded in the Cartesian "I think, therefore I am," the new education might instead be grounded in the southern African concept of *Ubuntu*: "I am, because we are."[9] We may treat the accumulation of private property with suspicion and instead emphasize shared decisions about the distribution of resources for the common good.

For example, we may think of a diploma not narrowly, as a ticket to a higher wage job, but more communally, as allowing entry into certain positions of trust within the neighborhood, positions that contribute to the well-being of everyone who lives there. Nothing prevents people's assemblies from convening and deciding that the youth of *this* community should satisfy particular agreed-on requirements for the status of "well-educated"—a community diploma. This is the underlying logic of traditional rites of passage, that the individual accepts certain teachings and practices tied chronologically to puberty: the social role involved in establishing a family or belonging to a clan, ideas about economic production and exchange, and about shared responsibilities within the collective. Our parallel diploma process may look at an individual's mastery of some body of knowledge—mathematics or music or historical research—both as indicating something about that individual and also as indicating something about the community from which that individual has emerged: the physical geographic community not as a place to escape from but as a site of self-healing and nurturing for future growth and for raising families. The term "parallel diploma" does not imply a concession; parallel institutions are a phase of insurrection, building strength until they can challenge and usurp the dominant power.

People in *all* communities think about collective values and always will. But in twenty-first-century America—apart from a few footholds—it is only in wealthy communities that the educational institutions vigorously reinforce *collective* interests. In expensive private schools or in some long-established elite public schools whose families are economically secure, there are traditions of communal investment in the community's children. Receiving a degree from one of these schools represents for students, their families, and members of the community not only the individual's achievement but something shared and worth preserving for future generations. Many of these students would not dream of escaping the community or its circumstances but are able to envision returning to raise their own children into a healthy and thriving adulthood. These are the schools with large endowments, whose faculty are largely drawn from its own alumni; the educational institution makes sense as a vehicle for social and cultural continuity.

But in most poor communities in twenty-first-century America, educational institutions are largely dissociated from the collective. Explicitly, the individual student is encouraged to get the most they can out of the institution, even to compete aggressively for the limited significant opportunities, and then to make use of whatever advantage they are able to win through their effort and talent to access something "higher" in the country's social, economic, or political hierarchy. The proof of this pattern of behavior is the tragic disappearance of many schools that once were sites of hope for poor and oppressed communities but that now have been razed or converted to some other purpose—condominiums or high-tech incubators for projects launched by young adults who grew up elsewhere. Education as a collective goal means nothing if it does not reinforce cultural continuity of some kind. And no enduring culture has yet been created that does not at least fantasize a geographic home.

Diplomas and credentials that reinforce the status quo function in many ways as currency—portable like cash and largely abstracted from the circumstances of production. Any mainstream diploma is taken to represent some abstract quantum of learning that matches what we pretend are roughly common expectations across the country. This abstraction intensifies in online courses, whereby a set of standards are represented as "information," "questions," and "answers" that students move through in varying degrees of electronic isolation (sometimes students communicate online during these courses with flesh-and-blood teachers or with other students, sometimes not). More and more, the acquisition of knowledge is independent of the social, physical, emotional, geographic, and material contexts of the learner or teacher. The wealthier the student, the more the material and social characteristics matter: wealthy families still pay large sums for their children to attend gorgeous fenced-off schools with small intimate classes, vast athletic fields, gymnasiums, studios, auditoriums, opportunities for trips abroad, and rituals that bind intergenerational students and alumni. But such experiences are increasingly unavailable to the poor and even to the middle class. If the state-mandated curriculum can be delivered electronically in a hardware and software environment and the students' mastery can be confirmed by their choosing the correct answers on the automatically scored and normed electronic test, why worry about the actual geographic or cultural environment?

The Pennsylvania Virtual Charter School, for example, is one of fifteen cyber charters in Pennsylvania. It has been operating since 2001 and collects close to $30 million of public funds annually to teach 2,500 students at a time. There is no physical campus. Twenty-one states allow for the creation of such cyber charters, and 75 percent of school districts in the country use online courses for "credit recovery" (earning credit for a course previously failed).

The project of education through peer-to-peer enterprises is very different. It is autochthonous, sprung from the earth. The physical situation of the young people in their geographic community is an important feature of their total acts. They see, hear, and touch each other. They smell the food cooking that will nourish their bodies, and they taste it, with culturally and individually idiosyncratic likes and dislikes. More and more, they grow their own food on their community's own land too. They sing songs, play instruments, dance, wrestle, run, bump into things, watch for cars, ride bikes and skateboards, get sick, get better, argue, tease. All this living, and much more, is not separate from learning but is an integral part of it.

Kwanzaa and the Fight Against Gentrification

In 1966 Pan-Africanist Maulana Karenga mined various African traditions to invent a new holiday that could be celebrated intentionally by Black people in America. The seven principles of Kwanzaa are excellent descriptions of the ethos of peer-to-peer youth enterprises that I am addressing.

Umoja (Unity): To strive for and maintain unity in the family, community, nation, and race.

Kujichagulia (Self-determination): To define ourselves, name ourselves, create for ourselves, and speak for ourselves.

Ujima (Collective work and responsibility): To build and maintain our community together and make our brothers' and sisters' problems our problems and solve them together.

Ujamaa (Cooperative economics): To build and maintain our own stores, shops, and other businesses and to profit from them together.

Nia (Purpose): To make our collective vocation the building and developing of our community in order to restore our people to their traditional greatness.

Kuumba (Creativity): To do always as much as we can, in the way we can, in order to leave our community more beautiful and beneficial than we inherited it.

Imani (Faith): To believe with all our heart in our people, our parents, our teachers, our leaders, and the righteousness and victory of our struggle.[10]

The Kwanzaa principles are a response to diaspora, and they envision a whole, an integral, not a collection of fragments. Current schools offer an image of individual escape from the "ghetto" or from the dysfunction of "laziness" and "ignorance." But our project sees the people as self-healing in the spirit of Kwanzaa: self-determining; primarily cooperative, not primarily competitive, in its economics; creative and spiritual, not extractive and materialistic; respecting and holding up the way we look out for each other; and committed to solidarity in the face of oppression, in the face of "divide and conquer."

The seven principles of Kwanzaa, or something very like them, are key to the development of a network of youth enterprises. We are constructing an education that answers to a people, however that people defines itself. We are not constructing an education that is rootless or disembodied.

Mindy Fullilove's book *Root Shock* on the epidemiological effects of urban renewal in the 1950s and '60s reminds us that the uprooting of the African kidnappings and the triangular trade was not a singular occurrence but repeats itself at all scales like a fractal pattern.[11] Between 1955 and 1965 most cities east of the Mississippi saw the ecology of Black communities pulverized to make room for the new federal interstate highways. Not coincidentally, this destruction followed immediately on the heels of the desegregation ruling in *Brown v. Board*.

A system of education is *not* located in the schools. This is an illusion of our current fragmentary, compartmentalizing, bureaucratizing political economy. A system of education is a way of weaving the strands of developing young lives into the already-existing and ever-changing fabric of a culture. This weaving involves all the aspects of human being: the sexual, emotional, spiritual, intellectual, communicative, aesthetic, natural, enculturated whole.

When whole communities are razed and the people in them displaced, one effect, Fullilove shows, is a rapid increase in morbidity and mortality, cancers, miscarriages, hypertension, and other physical illness. Another effect is the interruption of education as a *normal* process. Education becomes extraordinary, something to be fought for and struggled over, rather than something that emerges naturally from the ways of a people like green shoots in spring.

This constant uprooting is the condition of education for Africans in America and has been since the seventeenth century: education is something that must be struggled over, because education is tied to place, and being torn from a place interrupts organized learning. Slavery, virtual re-enslavement at the end of Reconstruction, the World Wars, and the mechanization of farming all caused huge displacements not freely undertaken by Black populations. Vast migrations caused by economic exploitation and war continue to cause similar displacements for millions of people around the world today.

Gentrification has the same effect as razing a Black or Brown community to make way for a highway. Being pushed out of a neighborhood interrupts housing, employment, and transportation, and it decimates the culture of a community. Part of that decimation is to make it very difficult to educate a next generation, not only because the schools are converted into condominiums but also because education is the process of helping children grow up into the society they actually live in, and when that society is experiencing fracture and dislocation, helping the children grow up becomes confusing and disturbing.

Our youth enterprises are, in part, an anti-gentrification strategy. Some green shoots are rising, and we organizers put a kind of netting or layer of straw over them, to stop them from blowing away and to allow those roots to grow and attach themselves to particular pieces of land. This netting is the structure of youth employment in knowledge work. It is a structure that is visibly distinct from the usual employment structures of capitalist America—not an employer coming in with tax breaks and quickly hiring a slew of interchangeable low-wage workers of color to serve the Whiter "creative class"; and not completely unsubsidized businesses that must succeed in an unprotected market. They are a network of knowledge-based youth collectives, economically and culturally protected to a certain extent, where value is generated from the ground up. When young people experience the benefits of collective self-determination—relatively stable income, the family cohesion that a little bit of income helps to foster, a sense of purpose and community—the network they have formed may be strong enough to resist developers' incursions.

Trusting Our Own Representations

The cognitive importance of a youth enterprise approach to education is that it creates public spaces in which students' experiences can be debated with reference to observations accessible to everyone who is physically present and who therefore has equal access to the experience and its representation. This is how people learn language, including the language of math and science.[12] People share an experience. They try to describe it. They agree on language that lets them use observation sentences[13] to decide whether a new experience is the same as or different from a familiar one. Their use of evidence and precise language is socially and culturally keyed to physical experiences in particular places. Location matters. They create site-specific knowledge that can nevertheless be abstracted and applied in new sites. Algebra Project peer-taught students, for example, run races in a playground, tell stories, and make drawings about the races before graphing distance and time. They are then willing to develop equations for speed out of their experience (speed = distance covered divided by time elapsed) and then to exchange the words for symbols ($m = \frac{\Delta y}{\Delta x}$ or $y = mx + b$) that can represent an infinite number of concrete experiences or relationships.

In contrast, the typical textbook or online course isolates a student in a virtual world where the only descriptions that count are the ones determined a priori by the platform developer or textbook writer. To whatever extent students are able to hold discussions about this abstract virtual world, they are only trying to agree on language that matches the developer's language. Their own descriptions are irrelevant. Such a method is cognitively disruptive and explains much of the current dysfunction in schools.

People tend to learn well when the language they use and hear around them captures the subtleties of their experiences in ways that are agreed on by their linguistic subgroup. Schools of poverty typically use language that either directly contradicts students' experience or that fails to capture the subtleties of that experience to students' satisfaction.[14] Many students who get failing grades in school nevertheless master volumes of technical information in contexts where a linguistic subgroup has succeeded in representing experiences accurately. Plenty of young people from poor communities have mastered hip-hop lyrics or spoken-word verses; video-game maneuvers, codes, or sequences; elements of fashion or hairstyles; transit routes; and relationship networks and histories. Little is understood in the technocratic world about how the very same student can have encyclopedic knowledge of one of these fields and be unable to explain which came first, the Revolutionary War or the

Civil War. I do not think that the answer is simply that one type of discourse is "interesting" or "relevant" and the other is not. I think the answer has more to do with a linguistic or cognitive experience: Where learning takes place easily, the student expects that language or representations will correspond to observations about the world in ways that a community generally agrees about. Hip-hop lyrics accurately describe idea-emotions that correlate to concrete experiences the students have had.[15] It's easy to remember the lyrics. (The music alone isn't enough. The periodic table translated into hip-hop lyrics doesn't work mnemonically unless the technical terms are embedded in a poetic context that is significant in its own right.)

The language of schools and textbooks, in contrast, is untrustworthy; it lacks credibility. The linguistic community (students, families, neighbors, many teachers) have not built a consensus about the utility of school language to capture the nuances of experience, and so it is hard to learn. Descriptions of the country's founding, for instance, include "All men are created equal" and also Thomas Jefferson's rape of his "property," Sally Hemings. How can language celebrating Jefferson be interpreted as trustworthy? The language of schools and textbooks is, in fact, often indistinguishable from the spectacularly unreliable and cruel languages of administrative bureaucracy. Denied food stamps or housing vouchers, or seeing loved ones psychologically tortured in courtrooms,[16] people in poor communities have too much experience with arbitrary signification in bureaucratic language to expect that it can be effectively learned, much less allowed to become a part of their most intimate conversations with themselves, the conversations necessary for substantive learning to occur.

For these reasons, one of the crucial aspects of peer-to-peer enterprises is the creation—extending over years—of linguistic communities that use agreed-on lexical, syntactic, and rhetorical forms to describe events and relationships in ways that can be observed and verified by anyone present. Young people engaged in any group activity develop their own ways of explaining and discussing what they do: features of a neighborhood ("the yellow house," "the hole in the fence"); people (by nicknames or physical characteristics—"black

Danny" or "red Danny"); actions (encoded in various local slangs for types of dance, fights, facial expressions); and, in fact, whole grammars. And all of these terms or grammars can be badly misused by outsiders, for example if you refer to some other house as "the" yellow house. This is to say that young people develop their own *technical* terms that are useful for very specific purposes and contexts and that are understood the same way by others in their local group. Similarly, hip-hop depends as art and communication on intricate lexical and grammatical understandings that are shared and agreed upon by practitioners and audiences.

There is absolutely no difference between this process of learning and creating a lexicon and grammar and the process of learning math and science, and young people must come to understand that they are already experts at the underlying process. Extending their expertise to the lexicon and grammar of mathematics requires only immersion in shared experiences and sustained exposure to practitioners with whom the learners identify and who are already expert in the language.

We know that language is integral to culture. We know that young people construct their own culture partly around the linguistic practices they embrace. Building strong youth-determined enterprises means supporting the experimentation, creativity, or even contrariness of youth languages. This process can be delicate in intergenerational contexts. Some teachers and organizers are understandably nervous about how authorities, a wider public, or even other teachers and parents may judge the language of the young people they work with. Sometimes the judgments are about grammatical "mistakes"—made orally or, especially, in writing: "How can these students (or teachers) care about education when they don't even speak or write correctly?" Sometimes the judgments are about "impropriety" or "disrespect." This particular concern provokes debates about respectability.[17]

Linguistic freedom is indispensable cognitively if we want young people in conditions of oppression to take on the task of mastering complex bodies of knowledge. Too much energy is wasted in buttoning down young tongues, energy that is then no longer available to be used in exploring the world. The buttoning down is instituted early in their school careers as a habit when four- or five-year-olds are corrected, although they are already using their own mother tongue with absolute mastery of the relevant forms. Very few students have the confidence to respect the intellectual seriousness of their own thoughts when they are constantly corrected for expressing them in the linguistic forms that first come to mind.[18] This is not a distinction between formal and informal expressions but, rather, between one kind of formality and another. Young people make choices in any given setting about whether to use the linguistic formalities of their peer group or to use other people's linguistic formalities, but there is no right or correct choice. Left to themselves, without moral judgment, in the context of the whole world and its history, they develop a purposeful blend of words and structures, reflecting a twenty-thousand-year-old mixture of influences. Spoken-word and hip-hop artists, for example, demonstrate every day how the very same words and phrases can be simultaneously erudite and colloquial.

Insulted by official standards presupposing their own culture's illegitimacy or otherness, many high school students intelligently reject dominant forms.[19] Hip-hop is, of course, the major force challenging the supremacy of normative school language in schools of poverty. Students attend to, study, comment on, and extend the language of their musical icons, of poets, and of their peers, understanding that the dominant society wants them to "code-switch" when they have to do something counted as serious by people with status and clout. But code-switching is the practice of deferring to dominant language forms where money, grades, or status are offered in exchange for deference. Don't use "be" as a finite verb in a job interview or a business environment; don't say "ain't" or use double negatives; don't use slang. These concessions to those with the power to hurt may be wise, or may be not, but however you see them, they come at a cost. Schools do not award academic credit for mastering hip-hop's language forms. Refusing to code-switch is usually punished severely. But encouraging students to develop habits of linguistic deference risks damaging children's self-identification as intellectually competent equals: "I don't speak properly. My family doesn't speak properly. My neighbors, my pastor, my peers don't speak properly. If I do speak properly, am I disloyal?"

The great majority of schools spread these kinds of thoughts like a constant and malicious innuendo. It might be the schools' worst crime. Provoking doubts about the status of your language provokes doubts about the status of your self. To say that students should learn to code-switch in academic or professional settings, or when they encounter people of a certain class or status in the power structure, is to take a political position. Code-switching is linguistic deference to the political status quo regarding who has economic and physical power. I am arguing that this political decision to defer, forced on very young children in school and imposed against their will on adolescents, has concrete negative cognitive effects.

The struggle for linguistic freedom has different dynamics in different communities, but it is one struggle. Users of American Sign Language (ASL) and native speakers of Spanish, Spanglish, African American English, Native American languages, Asian-Pacific languages, and every other language all have much to learn from each other. Some youth enterprises, among the many possible configurations, should take on language diversity directly as their value point. There are certainly markets for teaching ASL or Spanish or English. Where young people from different linguistic and cultural communities come in contact with each other, there are powerful economic arguments for paying them to teach each other their languages as a way to interrupt animosities, diversify labor pools, increase employment and entrepreneurial opportunities, and generally put otherwise marginalized people at the center of an enterprise.

This is no less true for the languages of math and science. I have found, teaching math in Baltimore public schools, that it usually takes two full years for a new group of students to completely trust the language I use in teaching. These specific forms, which I myself learned over years of work with Algebra Project pedagogy, are designed to give students control over their own mathematical representations. Initially, Algebra Project facilitators' language is seen by the students as strange and unwieldy—our questions or responses to students' remarks or observations, the way we describe our shared experiences, or what we write or draw seem to the students arbitrary, trivial, or unnecessarily complicated. Our questioning often aims at simple distinctions that can only be interpreted or resolved by looking at something in our public space and agreeing to a consensus description of what we observe. "Describe what you see" often turns out to be a confusing demand in a school mathematics setting. Why do I ask these kind of questions? students wonder. Why am I so confusing? Why don't I teach real math (meaning a set of repetitive problems on a worksheet)? My language cannot be trusted. Nor do students trust their own language in school. They do not believe that their spontaneous verbalizations will be adequate for talking about mathematics.

The Algebra Project does two things in the face of this problem: First, we have a peer or near-peer who is already experienced in math ask the students the same kinds of questions. The language isn't an adult teacher's alone; it is shared by a person from the culture and generation of the student. And second, we persist in asking these kinds of questions over years in a context of caring about the whole lives of the students—their families, their food, their transportation, their finances, their demands, their relationships, their conflicts, their culture. After about two years, students begin to trust and to use the language we use in teaching math. When we ask a question that seems too simple or too complicated or nonsensical, instead of assuming that there is no correlation between the question and their experience, the students now look for a correlation and trust that they may in fact find one that connects in an interesting way to other experiences they have had and to descriptions of their observations around which they have already developed a consensus. Learning accelerates rapidly from this point.

In the early phases of developing relatively autonomous student enterprises, many students may decide to code-switch. But as a network of youth enterprises emerges, the fertile linguistic interactions that occur in multiple crawl spaces will begin to acquire a political force of their own. A single person is often compelled to defer. But as young people become socially, economically, culturally, and politically organized, they also become able to represent themselves on their own terms. It could happen that their terms are actually more persuasive in other people's cultural contexts than the terms that dominated before.

At least twice in American musical history, the dominant culture has accepted and even welcomed expressions from outside the norm, first with the emergence of jazz from the tiniest, most remote Black crawl spaces into dominant commercial arenas and then with the emergence of hip-hop into a worldwide aesthetic and cultural idiom. If it had been up to the conservatories of music, of course, these cultural practices would never have gotten off the ground. Jazz and hip-hop were born in a network of out-of-the-way places fertile for invention. Eventually the body of work that developed in those places became powerful enough that the dominant culture cut its losses and deferred to them, rather than the other way around. A network of economically viable youth enterprises, already well underway, has a similar opportunity to change the language of the country as it grows in power.

As peer-to-peer youth language exchanges develop, it will be interesting to see how educational establishments react. Young people are interested in communication and adventure. Establishment language teachers tend to be interested in notions of correctness and rules as in-group or status markers. The Spanish of many young people in America is a concern to a certain kind of academic purist, and the English of many African-ancestored young people is no less a concern to another kind of purist. As these two linguistic communities of young people find more and more ways to talk with each other and to celebrate their own identities, amplifying their different but related cultural heritages, there will be a reaction. I can imagine teachers or administrators complaining about powerful youth language collectives: "They aren't even teaching each other correct grammar, and they're using words that don't even exist!" I look forward to the contest that will follow. That contest could only benefit the country's intellectual awareness of how language works. Bringing the workings of language to consciousness has always been a key act in any revolution. And shared language grounded in a particular place also grounds education.

Theater

An explosion of lyric poetry is well underway in the United States, a harbinger of the expansion of youth enterprises in dramatic arts. The immense accomplishments of poets and spoken-word activists from oppressed communities have enabled many artists to earn a living from the practice and teaching of their craft. Lyric poetry, as I am using the term, is a genre of relatively short first-person poems that are usually, though not necessarily, designed for a single performer or voice.

Often in cultural histories of varied places, periods of intense lyric development are followed by growth of larger dramatic performances and theater: a socially ambitious genre of longer pieces, usually employing multiple and conflicting voices and characters, attempting representations of difficult and unresolved tensions in the community, whether through comic, tragic, or some kind of ritual plot sequence from problem to climax to resolution.

As a society, we Americans have largely ceded the function of drama and theater to movies and television. Most young people do not attend live dramatic performances or act in them. It seems likely, however, that the immensely popular spoken-word and hip-hop performances that currently abound in the entertainment sphere will become jumping off points for a renaissance of live community-centered theater in the near future. Peer-to-peer youth enterprises based on teaching and staging dramatic productions will be crucial sources of new ideas and new relationships in this renaissance. A small but passionate cache of trained theater people are already waiting in the wings, so to speak, to assist such work. They are simply undercapitalized right now. We teachers and organizers should be planning to move capital toward them so they can set up youth theater companies using many of the resources that are currently being wasted on dead classrooms. Young performers, directors, playwrights, producers, and set designers should, of course, be paid.

The relative ease of video and music production due to technological advances can only benefit a renaissance of live theater. These performances can themselves begin—and have certainly already be-gun—in crawl spaces around the country. And by "theater" we refer not only to indoor locations with one kind of formality but also to any space—indoor or outdoor—that can be temporarily set apart from non-fictional routines and invested for a time with the magic of pretending that we are more than what we are and that the world is more than what it is. Modern western ideas of "audience" and "performer" are also likely to be further challenged by such youth enterprises. The drama of stance and experimentation with voice, diction, posture, and role are at the center of what it is to be human.

The significance of gathering large numbers of people in com-mon spaces in person, rather than virtually, is of course familiar in athletic, religious, musical, and political contexts. The meaning of rituals such as school graduations, weddings, and funerals is simi-larly centered in the shared physical experience of being together in the same place at the same time as a way of marking transitions to a next stage of life.

Dramatic theater adds the possibility of change to the ritual function of gathering in the same place at the same time. Rather than reuniting the community around already expected villains and heroes—the usual suspects—plays can gather the community around questions: Who is heroic? Who is vile? Can one be disguised as the other? Are our group identities static, or could they develop further? Are there ways to combine the virtues of both the hero and the villain in a new synthesis, or are there ways to exile the vices of both, purging the community without literally destroying hu-man life, because symbolic destruction in the play is compensation enough? How can we use symbolic creations—images, movements, melodies, myths—to simplify or promote some potential resolu-tions of social, class, generational, ethnic, or sexual tensions?

Music, art, film, television, social media, and both fiction and nonfiction writing address these questions for our current society. And there are undoubtedly ritualistic elements in our consumption of those forms. But live theaters as community institutions are likely to emerge, because people need public space to raise such questions in person. Live theater produced by young people who are paid for their labor could quickly develop a degree of technical excellence and create a shared understanding across generations of the power of youth intellect and creativity.

It is interesting to note in this context that two of the key groups in Baltimore's peer-to-peer youth enterprise network have participated significantly in proto-theatrical work for many years. Leaders of a Beautiful Struggle emerged out of public policy debate. Each debate enacts a miniature drama: protagonist, antagonist, argument, rebuttal, and a climactic decision of winner and loser at the end. The performances are public and personal. They spur dialogue and contests within the public audience, and they lead to revisions and restaging of arguments in response to previous debates, as the debaters grow and change.

The Baltimore Algebra Project has its own organic relationship to public performance. Its young members have generated a youth-determined culture around public political demonstrations: marches, rallies, takeovers of public hearings, die-ins. A crew with varied skills—oratory, spectacle, crowd management, personalizing public targets for dramatic effect, public relations—has grown up around this need to participate in public life. Each event is its own dramatic production. Anyone who wants to participate can have a part, but they have to learn to play it. The more demonstrations the students put on, the more they understand the technical skills needed to convey intended meanings to the audience.

The debate and demonstration protodramas are important in themselves, and a healthy society will develop many different types of dramatic ritual for negotiating tensions. Formal theatrical production will be just one of these many types of ritual, but I believe it will eventually be an important type, stimulating mass action.

Centering Disability Rights[20]

Students with disabilities and deaf and hard of hearing youth are also at the center of peer-to-peer youth enterprises. The goal is *not* to create "accommodations," adapting already-designed spaces, structures, and procedures as an afterthought. The goal is rather to understand the presence of people with many kinds of disabilities as constitutive of the structures and social forms of a humane educational system. Many families understand how the existence of someone with a disability enriches them by opening possibilities formerly closed off. Especially in considering questions of justice and injustice, being challenged to understand the humanity of each person leads to new social relations well beyond anything that could reasonably be called an accommodation. It is not only that someone in a wheelchair should have access to a building or that signage should have audio, visual, and tactile components, though these things are important aspects of justice. People with disabilities demand reconfigurations of power. Who decides? Who is entitled to represent? Who determines the value and worth of things? We have begun to get used to the idea of raising these questions of power in relation to race, ethnicity, language, gender, and sexual orientation. Educational contexts are outstanding places to push further on discussing questions of power in relation to abilities of all kinds.

There are huge opportunities within a wide range of youth organizations for youth who use American Sign Language—not only as interpreters but as second-language instructors. Young people of all ethnicities love signing since it incorporates movement, facial expression, and visual metaphor. Powerful paid roles for deaf and hard of hearing students as second-language instructors would undoubtedly improve their own self-perception and cognition as well. The lawyer and activist Talila Lewis also argues that police interactions with deaf and hard of hearing populations and other populations with disabilities are at the root of much more state violence than is commonly recognized.[21] Youth enterprises can take active roles in teaching police, prison guards, and bureaucrats about the needs of oppressed populations. These projects could be both lucrative and useful in reducing such violence.

Next, consider mental illness and the constraints it puts on daily life for youth in poor communities. The performing artist Son of Nun, a key member of Baltimore's activist community, points out that only one of many psychotherapists with whom he has worked on his depression has ever mentioned the topic of racism. Never has a therapist asked, "How did racism affect your day today?" or "How did patriarchy mess with your peace of mind since we last met?" Mental illness is not only a condition of the individual; mental illness is torture at the intersection of the body, the mind, and history. As Lester Spence, another Baltimore activist, puts it, therapy may be useful, but the challenge in front of us is not only a therapeutic challenge. It is also a challenge in political economy.[22]

The political economy of peer-to-peer youth enterprises tackles many structures of the dominant culture that exacerbate mental illness. Anxiety about cash income is an enormous trigger. The pressure in families short of cash for rent, a car, utilities, or food complicates adolescent social-emotional development and also affects the body's chemistry.[23] Wage stability for an adolescent can buy time. Support groups can be healing once trust has been built; the peer-to-peer youth enterprise builds in trusting relationships, so support groups formed within an enterprise start off ahead of the game. Arrangements that the group designs explicitly to support members suffering from depression or anxiety end up benefitting everyone, since everyone trying to survive under oppression has crises—family, social, emotional, romantic, financial—that require flexibility from the larger group. The ingredients of racism, sexism, homophobia, ageism, and ableism can be openly spoken of as part of a normal discourse, as opposed to ghettoizing the afflicted.

We have seen such supportive dynamics play out repeatedly in the Baltimore Algebra Project. From the outside, this process can seem frustrating and inefficient. A person in crisis leaves pieces of work undone or just doesn't show up. The argument here is not that the boss should show leniency or give the employee a break. The argument is, rather, that the collective, even if composed of very young people, can learn to build in a deep bench so that others can step up when crisis leaves a brother or sister faltering. Youth in poor communities anticipate crises. They have grown up expecting that the police, the landlord, an ignorant classmate, a neighbor, will mess with them. They know how suddenly depression or mania or psychotic voices or sexual aggression can intrude on their peace of mind whether from inside them or from a family member or just a stranger on the bus. So we can learn to make room for crisis intentionally in a way that lets the collective maintain its stability, even when an individual is thrown off balance. The stability of the collective, in turn, helps restore some equilibrium to the individual soul.

As a final example, extending the Virginia Department of Education's "I'm Determined" project, high school students of all abilities can be supported in organizing enterprises that teach other students how to plan their own educational programs, conduct their own IEP (individualized education program) meetings (federally mandated meetings for students with identified disabilities), and construct their own networks of support. Teachers can be taught by students how to understand learning differences as strengths, and young people can come to understand their roles as powerful and valued, rather than as marginal and troublesome.[24]

Who Teaches Younger Children?

Creating networks of peer-to-peer youth enterprises is a strategy for supporting young people who are enacting and demanding what they need for their own growing up. Rather than teachers, principals, districts, and the state making demands on them, students in peer-to-peer youth enterprises have learned to make demands on themselves, on each other, and on the adults around them for the support they need. This shift in adolescent roles from passive to active inspires younger children too. Younger children naturally imitate their big brothers and sisters, cousins and older children in the neighborhood, but it is the activity of those older exemplars, not their passivity, that is inspiring: running, dancing, playing ball, earning money, rapping, singing, doing hair, risking, branching out. Youth enterprises are an ideal place for younger children to observe teenagers playing active roles in more technical fields: making films, conducting experiments, teaching, performing, publishing, making things happen.

There is no good reason, in fact, that the school day for high school students should stay boxed into some 8:00 a.m. to 3:00 p.m. schedule. It makes much more sense to free up a part of many high school students' days so that they can find time to teach or help teach elementary and middle school children, drastically increasing the amount of one-to-one instruction younger children receive. Of course, they should fulfill this capacity by organizing themselves in teams or enterprises, with support from indigenous teachers, and they should get paid for this work. Elementary schools should be full of teenagers coteaching with highly skilled adults, supervising sports on playgrounds, helping produce plays and recitals, preparing snacks, gardening, reading, and playing all kinds of games with numbers just for fun. Why do we fight to make high school students attend classes we know are not helping them, instead of letting them be useful where they are desperately needed?

We currently treat older adolescents as large children, herding them into supervised schedules like first or second graders, controlling their whereabouts from early in the morning to mid-afternoon. Richer teens are allowed more independence in high school, frequently choosing their own courses or concentrations and having free periods during the school day, along with internships or special projects where they can be unsupervised and still trusted to learn. But in schools of poverty, electives are few, free time is treated as a scheduling error, and being without supervision during the school day is literally a punishable infraction. Of course, beyond the school day, adolescents are often entirely on their own, not only unsupervised but left to fend for themselves. The hypocrisy of supervision in schools is all about liability, not about the support young people need to thrive.

We would do better to understand adolescents as already beginning to enter the social, economic, and political world of adults. The time they devote to different parts of their lives should reflect this fact. We can imagine high school students learning many different things in many different contexts, sometimes being paid to teach or share a skill, sometimes receiving instruction from other young people employed for precisely that purpose. For example, a group of friends could start their day going to a local rec center for an exercise class taught by paid peers, cooling down afterwards at a student-run snack bar/teen-health hub that offers nutritious food, health information, referrals for students with worries, and free condoms. They might then go to their own jobs at a nearby elementary school where they do math with fifth graders. Their specialty, for example, might be geometric art, showing the amazing but relatively simple forms that can be constructed with a ruler and compass, or with dynamic software on a computer or phone. Their fifth graders could eventually share with parents how they make circles inscribed in triangles by finding the intersection of angle bisectors. The high schoolers might then make their way to their own high school math class, where, in addition to a skilled teacher, older or same-age peers help them learn new ways to explore circles and triangles at a more advanced level, using ideas from trigonometry, for example.

In the afternoon, one of the friends might attend play rehearsal, run by peers, where she is developing a role in an adaptation of Toni Morrison's *Beloved*, while another friend goes off to work on an oral history project with some paid youth researchers. A third member of this group goes to a scheduled stint at a worksite, learning from a peer how to do electrical wiring in a house that is getting renovated, supervised by a licensed electrician from the community. Another student, a strong athlete, ends the afternoon in a varsity practice and another, who loves basketball but isn't very good at it, plays in a youth-run intramural league. In the evening the friends watch a live-streamed political poetry slam managed for pay by some other young people at a cultural center downtown.

This picture of flexible teaching/learning/earning is already the reality for many teens, but parts of it are illicit or disconnected—squeezed into the time left over after school, not integrated with academic programs, erratic and dicey in pay, and all categorized under the rubric of "the hustle" at the margins of individualistic free enterprise. What is taught and learned in the hustle often has no future and is hard to build on. Peer-to-peer youth enterprises—even those operating in crawl spaces—organize energy in directions communities decide are worth the political and financial investment.

Devising Means to Change the System

This chapter has given just a preliminary sketch of the many opportunities that networks of youth enterprises open up: cultural, cognitive, economic, political, geographic. These kinds of opportunities are growing already in poor communities across the country, but we have found that the structure of youth enterprises can be helpful in creating bulwarks against attacks and pressures from the dominant society. Because peer-to-peer organizations create mini-societies that make sense to young people, their educational function is likely to be more satisfying and successful than the schools are able to match. And these mini-societies constitute organizing bases—base communities—from which insurgencies can be launched in an eventual struggle for collective ownership and control of public resources.

The vision projected in this book starts in particular local scenes and venues but ultimately is much larger and more extensive. As expertise develops within the local networks of youth enterprises and their corresponding base communities, power develops too. The growing power of these organizations in poor communities will lead to a clash for resources. At first, the small-scale experimentation with youth entrepreneurship strikes the powerful as a handy diversion, reinforcing neoliberal doctrines of self-help and privatization. Liberal do-gooders are delighted, too, by the guilt-reducing spectacle of young people of color having fun and learning useful skills. But it takes only a little genuine empowerment in places where oppressed young people congregate for them to start doing what many adults don't want them to do: make demands for radical social, political, and economic rearrangements to meet their needs. And even a relatively small network of youth enterprises and base communities will be powerful enough to compel sufficient rearrangement that the enterprises can be sustained and expanded.

Our experience has been that the dominant culture will accommodate such demands while youth-led enterprises are still small. The tiny Baltimore Algebra Project, for example, still receives hundreds of thousands of dollars in public funding each year to employ young people, even though those same young people have taken over school board meetings, organized boycotts of test days, performed a citizen's arrest of the state superintendent of education, blocked traffic to demand educational justice, and stymied the governor's attempt to construct a new $100 million youth jail. Young people teaching math to their peers have earned their insurgency, as Bob Moses puts it. By the time the alarm bells go off in the dominant system, these enterprises may be too strong to stop. A network of peer-to-peer enterprises supported by the rich vernacular culture of Baltimore's base communities will soon be able to tear off a larger piece of the economic pie for their own sustenance, rather than letting it all slip away to the Whiter, richer portions of the state and to the multinationals.

These larger battles are down the road but not very far. Unions will need to recognize a broader definition of "teacher," so that not only teachers in traditional classrooms but also mentors, skilled community members willing to take on apprentices, cooks, carpenters, and artists in neighborhoods are all understood as providers and guarantors of public education. The political economy of education will have to change to make room for new roles in how we bring up our children.

But the crucial first step is for a substantial number of young people to get themselves organized. They are unlikely to succeed at this goal if the economics aren't right, so we must find ways for them to earn some cash doing work that is meaningful to them. And they must have sufficient power and control of the particular circumstances in their local groups that they get a taste for what successful struggle feels like, how it shifts their relationships to each other, to the larger world, and in fact shifts the interior dialogue they are each having with themselves as they construct their identity.

These are powerful ideals, but they are not far-fetched. Radical teachers and organizers have witnessed this process many times. Given the dead end offered to young people by the larger society in today's world, the process of autonomous self-organization among oppressed youth is likely to accelerate. We adults should see how we can make ourselves useful. Support positive youth initiatives, even when we disagree with the particulars. Ask questions, but don't take power. Help figure out transportation and take care of some food. Make sure money gets into the young people's pockets and create good jobs for the twenty-to-thirty-year-olds who are committed to this base-building work. Ward off opportunists coming from outside the community looking to make a dime or to build their resumes. Challenge hypocrisy in the dominant power structure.

> In order for us as poor and oppressed people to become a part of a society that is meaningful, the system under which we now exist has to be radically changed. This means that we are going to have to learn to think in radical terms. I use the term *radical* in its original meaning—getting down to and understanding the root cause. It means facing a system that does not lend itself to your needs and devising means by which you change that system.[25]

These words of Ella Baker put the program in its simplest terms: young people in poverty face a system that does not lend itself to their needs. They are capable of devising the means to change that system, and they have already begun this work in groups, associations, collectives—new forms of social organization that first meet their needs in miniature, networking with similar groups as their power grows. If we can forestall catastrophic interruptions to this already well-developed process (avoid war, for example, or ecological meltdown), growing up in such networked groups will *be* the education of the latter twenty-first century. Families will bring their children up into viable social and economic cultures without needing to trust in the goodwill of outside benefactors for teaching, employment, financing, or legitimacy. Our lives will still be full of joy and striving, tragedy and trouble, but we will look to ourselves and our people—as we define "our people"—for the forms we need to raise our children into adulthood. This process is under way already; it is unlikely to end anytime soon.

CHAPTER 6

Accountability, the National Student Bill of Rights, and the Legacy of Struggle

Accountability from the Bottom Up

In the long run, resistance is not enough. Survival also requires creation. The youth enterprises I have described are pragmatic creations that reconfigure our human energy, establishing new forms of relationship. The aim of the youth enterprises is not to close the so-called achievement gap. The aim is to create more life. No child lives in comparison to another child and certainly not in comparison to another child's "achievement." Each of us lives only for ourselves and for those around us, human and nonhuman. Being alive is not "in comparison to" but "in ethical relation to."

Socialist and anarchist theory has long pointed out the alienating effects of money, but we have had an inadequate analysis of the negative effect of the currency of schools: tests and grades. Historically, the use of numerical grades in schools closely followed the development of industrial economies and the alienation of labor through wage slavery.[1] Modern systems of academic grading on one hand and wage labor on the other are two sides of the same coin. School can be exactly as boring and life-draining as the labor we undertake only for pay.

We are building a parallel political economy of youth enterprises as a location for creative insurgency. As part of this work, testing and grading as a system of alienating transactions should be countered by a parallel evaluative medium suited for our purposes. The "brightest" students are not at Harvard or Yale or Stanford. They are not at Howard or Spelman or Morehouse. They are all over the country, in every nook and cranny, on every corner, in every trailer park, under bridges, rotting in jails, sitting up at night with little siblings or sick grandparents. It is an absolute error to think that the measures of the education system correlate to anything other than the good fortune of fitting for one reason or another into the measures of the education system. Intelligence, giftedness, ability are everywhere, in every home. The vast majority of human gifts elude our measures. But it is comfortable to congratulate a neighbor when their son or daughter wins admission to a magnet school or a gifted program, and it would seem ungenerous not to. So the view that abilities are inequitably distributed, that they are scarce and governed by the laws of scarcity, is quite unshakeable in our time.

Let those who wish to do so continue to think that the brightest students are at Harvard. Let them believe that the magnet schools truly attract the most intelligent and capable young people. Meanwhile, we will go about the business of measuring what we value, not valuing what we measure. We do not need to measure one child against another. Instead we will measure the circumstances in which children grow up. Do those circumstances offer what children need so that their gifts will be revealed, so that they can take part in the country's life as equal members of one society? We can be confident that when those circumstances are realized, it will be obvious that the brightest students saturate our neighborhoods, filling every street and road with genius. Every school, every place of teaching and learning will be potentially enviable, a place where any parents would feel lucky to send their child.

One possible medium for measuring the circumstances that are the birthright of our children is the National Student Bill of Rights. NSBR is a list of fifteen rights demanded by young people across the country who are loosely connected through the biennial Free Minds, Free People conference sponsored by the Education for Liberation Network. EdforLib originated in the early 2000s out of work by Charles Payne, Tara Mack, and Thomas Nikundiwe to connect radical educators and young people teaching and learning in traditions of struggle against oppression. The fifteen rights in the

National Student Bill of Rights emerged from discussions of the meaning of national citizenship conferred by section 1 of the Fourteenth Amendment: "All persons born or naturalized in the United States, and subject to the jurisdiction thereof, are citizens of the United States and of the State wherein they reside." This Citizenship Clause of the US Constitution effectively nullified Justice Taney's 1857 ruling in *Dred Scott* that the class of persons whose ancestors were brought violently to the United States from Africa were not citizens and had no rights. By virtue of the Fourteenth Amendment, African Americans become Constitutional persons, liberated from their earlier condition as Constitutional property.

But the question remains: What do young people need in order to fully exercise their citizenship? An education? Yes, but what are the actual conditions in the twenty-first century that will result in a quality education for all young people? In many places around the country, the National Student Bill of Rights and other articulations of similar ideas are beginning to be used as organizing tools to advance this issue. It is becoming more and more clear, for example, that homelessness and nutrition must be addressed partly because of their educational effects. Young people understand this necessity viscerally, and so students in Baltimore, for example, argue that healthier and more plentiful school food is a right that they already possess, one that is not being honored. As of this writing, legislation is currently being prepared in the US Congress, with the help of the Algebra Project and other groups of organized adults and young people, to create comprehensive enforcement of the Fourteenth Amendment's guarantee of citizenship as it relates to the building blocks of education.

The list of rights below was created over many years of discussion among young people of color from Baltimore, Providence, Philadelphia, Boston, Atlanta, New Orleans, Oakland, San Francisco, Denver, Chicago, Salt Lake City, Albuquerque, Los Angeles, New York, Jackson, Detroit, Milwaukee, and elsewhere. It is a response to the question: What do we need in order to learn everything that we want to learn? Understanding the facts of their own lives, these young people identified barriers and freedoms that go far beyond the usual constraints of school systems' curricula and supports.[2]

National Student Bill of Rights for All Youth

Right to Free Public Education: The right to a free public education shall not be denied or abridged on account of race, gender, disability, ethnicity, religion, poverty, actual or perceived sexual orientation, gender identity, place of residency, or immigration status.

Right to Study Curriculum That Acknowledges and Addresses Youth's Material and Cultural Needs: Students and youth shall have the right to study curriculum that acknowledges and affirms the ongoing struggle of oppressed peoples for equality and justice, and that addresses the real, material, and cultural needs of their communities.

Right to Safe and Secure Housing: Students and youth shall have the right to safe and secure housing.

Right to Free Public Transportation: Students and youth shall have the right to free public transportation for the purposes of education, employment, family and community needs, or recreation.

Right to Physical Activity and Recreation: Students and youth shall have the right to physical activity and recreation of high quality regardless of their wealth, poverty, or place of residence.

Right to Safe and Secure Public Schools: Students and youth shall have the right to safe and secure public school facilities of equal quality regardless of wealth, poverty, or place of residence.

Right to Free Health Care: Students and youth shall have the right to free health and dental care, including quality public health and preventive care.

Right to High-Quality Food: Students and youth shall have the right to healthy, high-quality food regardless of wealth, poverty, or place of residence.

Right to Employment: Students and youth shall have the right to employment, to support themselves while they are in school and college.

Right to Free Daycare for Children: Students and youth with children of their own shall have the right to free day care for their children.

Right to Free College Education: Students and youth shall have the right to free college education.

Right to Freedom from Unwarranted Search, Seizure, or Arrest: Students and youth shall be secure from arbitrary police searches and seizures and from arbitrary arrests and detentions without warrants.

Right to Restorative Justice and Peer Evaluation: Students and youth shall have the right to establish systems of restorative justice in schools and communities, shall not be excluded from educational opportunities except by a jury of their peers, and shall not be charged for crimes as adults until the age of eighteen.

Right to Arts Education: Students and youth shall have the right to participation in arts, music, dance, drama, poetry, and technology of high quality regardless of wealth, poverty, or place of residence.

Right to Reproductive Health: Students and youth have the right to make informed decisions about their own bodies and reproductive abilities and to have those decisions respected free from judgment or coercion.[3]

The Right to Transportation 24/7

Each of these rights should be carefully studied and discussed. They emerged from intense suffering and joy in the actual lives of young people attempting to learn under conditions of oppression. I want to look briefly at the right to transportation as an example, and then consider the entire Student Bill of Rights as an accountability tool for a new system of education.

In the typical suburban American high school, many juniors and seniors drive themselves to school in their own car or in a family car. Suburban White students, especially, have good access to their own transportation, or to transportation provided by their family or their school system. By contrast, very few of Baltimore's African American students drive themselves to school. Only special education students in Baltimore use dedicated yellow buses. The majority of students take public transportation, subsidized for trips to and from school, on school days only, before 8:00 p.m. But Baltimore's public transportation system is not so wonderful. Many trips take more than ninety minutes, and often buses pass students by because they are full or simply because drivers don't care to stop for middle and high school passengers. Most city high school students do not yet have drivers' licenses because of economic barriers, and the relatively few who have a license can't afford a car. A family with no economic cushion must use its vehicles transporting someone to work rather than leaving a car sitting idle at school all day.

Educationally, there are important ramifications to this inequality between wealthier and less wealthy students. Poor-quality public transportation results in many hours a week spent in transit for students who depend on the bus to get to school, and this mode of transportation subjects students to all kinds of harassment, sexual and otherwise, or to the physical danger of getting to buses or waiting at bus stops. Students who can afford to drive cars have more time and opportunity to spend on homework, athletics, internships, employment, music lessons, or other pursuits with educational effects. Self-image and a sense of agency are important determinants of academic achievement and are greatly enhanced by having a car. Students with cars can go out with friends or on dates. They can help their families with errands or get across town to carry groceries for their grandmothers. These positive independent roles build skill and confidence and have cognitive effects. When arrangements meet your needs and make some sense, the structure of schooling for future success is easier to tolerate, and you can likely learn what people are trying to teach you. But for a student waiting in the cold at six in the morning for a bus that is still going to make him late for school, a student who is unsure of how he will get home after practice because his bus ticket will have expired and his mother will already be working the late shift, a student who is hungry and has no money in his pocket to get something to eat and is worried about a math test he should have studied for last night but didn't because he had to lug the family's clothes to the laundromat while he helped his little brother with homework—that student is less likely to tolerate the doubtful promises of schooling.

The point is not that a guarantee of free public transportation for students twenty-four hours a day, seven days a week would relieve all the difficulties of poverty. The point is that free transportation would be an arrangement that makes sense to our students, an arrangement that might seem designed to meet their actual needs. They might still think a car would be better, but there is also a certain sense of independence and freedom from anxiety that comes from having an unlimited transportation pass, as anyone who has ever bought one can verify. The idea is not just to get to and from school but to be able to access all the opportunities that transportation makes accessible: parks, sports events, concerts, friends, family, museums, festivals. The expense is not prohibitive in western economies: Germany, for example, already uses a similar system. Free transportation for young people in the United States would also result in many more of them being out and about, generating positive social interaction through greater awareness of opportunities and encounters with new ideas. All renaissances historically are ignited by the mingling of populations through increased travel and intercultural contact. The benefits of local travel are not less powerful than travel on national and international scales.

This extended annotation on transportation is meant to illustrate how the rights in the National Student Bill of Rights have emerged from students' intimate experiences and reflections. This is not merely a wish list. It is an analysis of the conditions under which young people feel they could thrive, despite their poverty—the conditions under which they might sense that they are actually powerful and not oppressed.

Political Demands in a Democracy

The purpose of this chapter is to describe an accountability system suited to the parallel political economy of youth enterprises. The accountability system of the current educational economy is the system of testing and grading. Teachers, principals, and administrators are ranked and rated based on students' test scores and graduation rates. Students are "held accountable," as well, by grades and test scores until the accountability of wages and salaries, promotions and unemployment, takes over in the "real world."

The theory of tests, grades, and money as instruments of accountability is simplistic: effort must be incentivized by extrinsic rewards. People will act properly if they are punished by low grades or unemployment when they resist institutional demands and rewarded with high grades and high wages when they conform. We are used to seeing this theory dressed up with the moralizing of merit, duty, caring, and the dignity of work. But there is really no other way to interpret the volumes of policy debates on holding teachers accountable through "value-added metrics," for example, or the nearly infinite number of lectures adults give children on "keeping up their grades." "Conform and you will be rewarded" is our current theory of accountability.

In many contexts, this theory reflects the way the system works. It is unhelpful, however, when it is applied in contexts where it doesn't hold. And it is an immoral theory when it functions as a lie, as it does within the structure of capitalist White supremacy. Rewards and punishments are distributed unfairly in present-day America, and so the lessons of accountability don't get learned, because they are unlearnable. Tearing down this system would not be a bad thing, but we focus instead on building up a different system of accountability.

A National Student Bill of Rights looks at accountability from below. Rather than judge the quality of a school on the basis of test scores, it asks, why not judge the quality of a school on whether its students are studying curriculum that helps them meet their material and cultural needs, on whether they are well-fed and well-housed, on whether they have good transportation, art, athletics, jobs if they need them, access to health care and contraception, peaceful ways to resolve disputes, and protection from arbitrary police powers?

Many people think schools can't be accountable for all those things. They aren't equipped. No. But the larger society can be and ought to be accountable. And the young drafters of the National Student Bill of Rights have intelligently argued that the rights are both necessary and sufficient conditions for studying and learning. Without food, housing, transportation, employment, relevant curriculum, health care, and justice, learning will continue to be sporadic and unevenly distributed. With those things in place, learning is inevitable.

Practicing the National Student Bill of Rights

NSBR is not utopian. I once asked a group of young people in the offices of the Baltimore Algebra Project, "Which of these rights described in the NSBR do your schools practice?" The answer was none of them. The curriculum is irrelevant; if you are sick, the school doesn't care; if you are homeless, the school rarely knows; the food is awful; whether you have a job is not the school's concern; and the police search you every day without a warrant.

Then I asked which of the rights were practiced in the Baltimore Algebra Project office, and the answer was all of them. We earn money here; when someone can't afford food, we share or the organization pays; everyone looks out for each other to make sure we have a safe way to get home; we study our own cultural history and understand that even math is a part of our culture; when someone has a housing problem they can sleep at a coworker's house or at the office itself in an emergency; we settle our differences by dialogue in circles; and someone who has children can bring them to the office anytime, because it's a baby-friendly place.

Being human, in other words, comes naturally to us. We are able to meet our own needs, individually and collectively, when we enter a cultural space conducive to being human. It is only in cultural spaces that are anti-human that we find it hard to get ourselves together and act effectively.

Although young people feel alive and human in the mini-culture that they have created and are preserving for themselves and for the next generations, they nevertheless continue to be nearly overwhelmed by the difficulties they face in the larger world. Their lives are almost impossible. Death, disease, violence, brutality, misogyny, homophobia, poverty, homelessness, racism, and hunger are their daily companions. The question they must face is how to widen the circle of caring that they know through their own experience is possible.

The strategy is therefore to teach about the rights that young people in poverty should have and to organize a demand that school systems, cities, states, and the country should be accountable for respecting those rights. Youth enterprises are one important avenue for developing such a demand, because they are well-suited to the required structure of an *earned* insurgency. Demanding free public transportation and healthy food as basic human rights is radically different from learned helplessness. In their peer-to-peer enterprises, young people make demands on themselves and on their peers: to perform real labor; to create high-quality intellectual, cultural, and material products; to share what they know effectively and pragmatically; to build social infrastructure throughout their community by practicing their rights and responsibilities as participants in a healthy organization. Making these demands on themselves and on their peers earns them the right to also make demands on the larger society. The structural principle is not asking for handouts but is, rather, a well-argued proposal for new allocations of society's collective resources, material and cultural, so that the needs of the entire collective can be met.

The cultural and human resources of the poor are vastly underemployed and should contribute much more than they do now to the common good. The cultural and material resources of the wealthy are walled off in ways that have led many people to a spiritual and cultural desert. The poor and the rich could both contribute much more than we do now to the well-being of the whole, if our goal was actually the maximizing of our collective product.[4]

Accountability for particular pieces of learning—reading, history, science, math—is best addressed locally by people who actually know the children involved. The idea that a local community lacks competence to ensure that all its children can read or do math rests on a mistaken colonial assumption about the cultural backwardness of the community. Actually, it is not difficult to decide when a child knows how to read or solve equations or research a topic in biology or history. In a trusting and confident community, you just ask them to show you.

And the theory that accountability for things like "basic reading" and "basic math" could be purchased through a system of testing, punishment, and credentialing from outside the community has produced fifty years of data proving the theory false. All learning is contextual. There is no basic reading or basic math but only reading, math, art-making, and research for human purposes in human communities. The very body of knowledge that schools claim to teach emerged not from schools but from human need, from the ordinary activity of people solving problems to make sensible and inspiring arrangements for themselves.

Let each community work out its own accountability structure for what it wants its children to know. But organize young people to demand on local, state, and national scales that the larger society respect their right to a democratic education and to all the conditions that will make such an education materially and practically possible.

The Ideals of the Country versus the Interests of the States[5]

Finally, I would like to address an objection to the peer-to-peer youth enterprise strategy. In the process, I will be able to situate the use of the NSBR as an accountability tool within the centuries-long trajectory of the Black freedom struggle.

The objection I have encountered is that because our peer-to-peer enterprises are based for now mostly in the private sector—that is, they are mostly not subsumed under the current governance structure of the public school systems—they are likely to be co-opted by proponents of market-based educational reform. What is to stop corporations from coming into poor communities to run educational enterprises that compete for the public dime? In fact, don't they already do this, sucking money out of public schools in the process?

It will be useful to compare the example of charter schools to the strategy of peer-to-peer youth enterprises. There is a left wing and a right wing of the charter school movement, and they have as much in common as anarchists and libertarians. The left wing wants local communities to be free of mainstream constraints so that liberating pedagogies can create power for oppressed families. The Betty Shabazz International Charter Schools in Chicago, founded by Carol Lee and Haki Madhubuti, for example, came out of the Black Power and Black Arts traditions of the 1960s. They are controlled by and answerable to the South Side Chicago community. In contrast, the KIPP charter schools, with hundreds of schools across the country, unaccountable to local populations, are heavily underwritten by the Walton Family Foundation, strong opponents of teachers' unions and local control. The right wing answers to its investors, who claim to operate as trustees for poor communities. Hardly any of their multi-billion-dollar annual budgets trickle down as wages to the families they are said to serve. The funds go instead to people outside the community.

In some respects the corporate right-wing charter movement can be thought of as more powerful than the left-wing charter movement. Certainly, the neoliberal charters have much more money behind them, access to politicians, and influence on educational policy. Because of these advantages, many education activists who fight against neoliberal oppression warn that charter-like education reforms will be overwhelmed by corporate power, undermining their radical anti-racist egalitarian strategies.

The peer-to-peer youth enterprise idea might be included in this danger zone. Youth enterprises are structured as eventual competitors for the funding and authority currently held tightly by public school systems. Like charter schools, the youth enterprises could be susceptible to right-wing versions, underwritten by corporate interests looking to siphon off public funding into private coffers distant from the communities involved. But let's look again at the charter school strategy. Fundamentally racist, the neoliberal charter proponents identify urban school districts as problematic because they are full of what the charter proponents see as incompetent teachers and administrators. These supposed incompetents just happen to also be people of color. White well-connected "innovative" "game-changers" leapt on the neoliberal bandwagon by circumventing local school districts with direct appeals for charters from state governments, that is, from bastions of White supremacy. Just three months after Hurricane Katrina, for example, the State of Louisiana passed legislation to take control of almost all public schools in New Orleans, waived regulations to make charter schools easier to open, and forced the dismissal of 7,500 mostly African American New Orleans teachers and administrators.[6]

This is, after all, the fundamental dynamic of American educational politics: state governments preserve White privilege, sometimes relinquishing nominal control of hollowed out urban areas to people of color. Of course, financial resources are inadequate to support the population of cities abandoned during White flight, but the effects of poverty can be blamed on the incompetence of Black and Brown officials rather than on the institutional racism of the underlying economic and political structures. Urban districts in forty-five states have sued state governments for inadequate educational financing—governments controlled by both Democrats and Republicans.[7] Sometimes urban districts win, sometimes they lose. But the lawsuits are in either case symptoms of the structure of America in our cold Civil War. Power and wealth are still held mostly by White people who enforce geographic segregation through property rights and so ensure better access to education for their own children.

Neoliberal charter operators overwhelm local districts by using well-capitalized networks to influence state-level authorities, for example by attacking teachers' unions or propping up predominantly White schools of education through lucrative alternative certification programs. Radical charter schools take no part in this institutional re-inscription of racism. But they also see their power begin to fade vis-à-vis the big corporate players. The corporate players, of course, are not transforming education. They are extracting wealth, siphoning public funds into the pockets of the already wealthy, leaving very little academically or socially in the community to show for it.

The tactic of racists appealing to state governments is not new in American history. Slaveholding states only signed on to the Constitution of 1787 after it was agreed that their relatively underpopulated states would receive oversized voting power through the three-fifths clause and disproportionate representation in the US Senate and electoral college. During the Civil War, the Confederate states asserted that their prerogatives regarding ownership of human beings would not be constrained by federal authority. And more recently, voting rights and other civil rights have been—and continue to be—denied by state authorities despite the passage of the Civil War amendments. The appeal to states' rights continues to be made today in openly racist ways.

Charter legislation that allows state authorities to circumvent or undercut Black and Brown power in local educational jurisdictions should be seen as part of this same racist history. But notice the complicated role the federal government plays in alternately supporting and opposing the racist demands of the states. On one hand, the federal government has created structures that enable the wealthiest and Whitest to make advantageous arrangements for themselves at the expense of the common people. The Supreme Court decision *Rodriguez v. San Antonio* (1972), for example, protected de facto segregation in Texas by insisting that only states, not the federal government, could determine educational funding structures.

On the other hand, the federal government has sometimes been compelled to mobilize an idealistic power in defense of individual and group freedoms, even when those freedoms clash with the wishes and intentions of White supremacy. The Civil War is one example of the federal government's siding, despite huge internal contradictions, with the most vulnerable. The Civil War amendments, labor laws, the New Deal, Presidents Eisenhower and Kennedy sending federal troops and marshals to defend school integration, the Civil Rights and Voting Rights Acts, protections for the rights of women, disability rights, and a whole series of federal court rulings are other examples where the federal executive, legislative, and judicial branches have stood in opposition to many state governments and to the private interests of the wealthy. In each of these instances, federal authorities acted only when compelled by the force of popular insurgencies. Certainly, these various protections are incomplete, contradicted by innumerable other federal actions, and have often excluded people of color, women, undocumented and LGBTQ people, and people with disabilities. The important point here, however, is that the federal government has historically been leveraged by oppressed people as a countervailing power to the racism and patriarchy of the states.

President Obama betrayed this legacy in relation to charter schools and neoliberal education reform when his Department of Education imposed punitive test-based formulas on schools through the Race to the Top grant program of 2009. His anti-radical pro-capital instincts seem to have pushed him toward hoping that the states would do the right thing, even though they were systematically eliminating voting rights for people of color and even though they continually prove themselves uninterested in promoting educational justice. But there is still time for a larger national battle over education in which the federal government might be compelled to take the side of justice once again.

One such opportunity will arise during the structuring of peer-to-peer youth enterprises as components of a new education system. If they are corporatized and given over to regulation by state governments, they will become new vehicles for extractive economics like charter schools. But we who believe in freedom will fight for a different legal structure, one protected by appeal to the federal rights of a constitutional people, as opposed to the racially constrained caste system imposed by unrestrained state governments.

Participants in peer-to-peer youth enterprises see themselves as inheritors of a legacy of struggle, not as helpless minorities whose interests are always subordinated to the interests of the wealthier White people who control state legislatures. Those legislatures continue to assert their prerogative in abrogating the rights of people of color—through incarceration, judicially sanctioned police violence, debtors' prisons, denial of the vote, denial of the fundamental human rights to food and shelter and employment, omissions of due process, and sharecropper education. Forty-five states have been sued by students or their families in urban districts; but no state has yet been willing to accept responsibility for the material and social conditions that make education possible for all the children within their borders. They are no more capable of meeting this challenge on their own than Southern states are capable of preserving voting rights without federal oversight. But federal interventions can result and have resulted from oppressed people insisting on their status as constitutional persons, bringing to the surface the difference between what the country professes and what it permits. The legislation mentioned earlier to enforce the Fourteenth Amendment's guarantee of citizenship by underwriting the National Student Bill of Rights is one possible example of such a federal intervention.

In order to develop as networks capable of resisting corporate power, youth enterprises will need a theoretical understanding of the federal/state dynamic. The privatizers—not just charters but also web-based and transnational educational services of all types—pressure public schools to feed them cash by promising to return high quality education as the states define and credential it. I do not deny that the pro-corporate aspect of the federal government completely supports this scam. But young people should define education in their own terms, as free persons who claim the right to determine their own futures, submitting for payment the promissory note that Dr. Martin Luther King Jr. spoke of, the one that guarantees life, liberty, and the pursuit of happiness, the one the country still returns with the stamp "insufficient funds." Young people are trying to make a demand *on the country* that their material conditions must be stable and that learning must be connected to their cultural history. This is their right as constitutional people, and they are working to earn the attention of the country by developing their insurgency on the basis of their intellectual and cultural accomplishments.

I use the language of personhood rather than of citizenship because it is clear that the right to education belongs to everyone, including documented and undocumented immigrants, as fully protected people under the law. This distinction is included in the Constitution of 1787 and is crucial to the Fourteenth Amendment: "nor shall any State deprive any person of life, liberty, or property, without due process of law; nor deny to any person within its jurisdiction the equal protection of the laws." The distinction was as relevant when this language was drafted in the 1860s as it is today: not only citizens but all persons living in this nation are equally protected by the law.

Youth enterprises are intended to advance education as a quality of our national, and also of our international, ideal. Education undergirds the right to vote, the right to free speech, and the exercise of religion, and it grounds the power to establish justice. When young people and the older people who gather around them begin to fight to preserve and expand their network of youth enterprises that pay wages through knowledge work, they will be fighting for their right to participate in the constitution of their own way of life.

Some people may question this appeal to American ideals, but those ideals remain powerful both symbolically and pragmatically. Molefi Kete Asante, a key proponent of Afrocentric education, pointed out in this regard that W. E. B. Du Bois may have misanalysed the double consciousness he experienced. For Du Bois, the "two-ness," as he called it, came from being both a Negro and an American. But for Asante, the two-ness is not inside him but rather reflects the double nature of the United States. The federal government has acted both as the vehicle of torture and oppression and—through its constitutional principles—as a weapon for justice and liberation, the only weapon, in fact, strong enough to put down slavery and Jim Crow.[8]

Bob Moses asks us to understand the Preamble to the

Constitution not as someone else's writing or agreement but as an act that we ourselves can perform for our own purposes and in our own way: "*We the People of the United States* [all of us, documented and undocumented, not "We the Citizens"⁹ but "We the People," all to varying extents both free and bound], *in order to form a more perfect union* [admitting both imperfection and hope], *establish justice* [the demand of the Movement for Black Lives], *insure domestic tranquility* [to be free from threats and violence by our neighbors, coworkers, police, and ICE], *provide for the common defense* ["common" meaning shared by all, not just defense of the propertied], *promote the general welfare* [benefitting every family], *and secure the blessings of liberty to ourselves and our posterity* [establishing education as central to the possibility that our children will know how to fight for liberation], *do ordain and establish* [fundamentally an act of purpose and intention] *this Constitution for the United States of America*." Whose country is it? Who defines what it will be? Why not us? These questions highlight the abstraction of the notional "country" called America. A country is an abstraction, but we should not slip into the error that it is therefore beyond our control. We are able to define what is important for ourselves.

Rude and Imperfect Cellars

Africans in America have always defined learning to be important. In her study *Self-Taught*, Heather Williams describes the efforts of enslaved and recently liberated people to acquire literacy in the American South of the nineteenth century. Example after example points to their insistence that they would educate themselves. Slave owners forbade, outlawed, and punished literacy efforts because the slaves' ignorance served the masters' purposes. But thousands refused to defer to these restrictions and instead found each other and found ways to read. "Rather than simply waiting for help to come," Williams writes about the freedpeople just after the Civil War, "they used what learning they had to begin to teach."

A Freedman's Bureau superintendent describes this phenomenon: "Not only are individuals seen at study, and under the most untoward circumstances, . . . but in very many places I have found what I will call 'native schools,' often rude and very imperfect, but *there they are*, a group, perhaps, of all ages, *trying to learn*. Some young man, some woman, or old preacher, in cellar, or shed, or corner of a Negro meeting-house, with the alphabet in hand, or a torn spelling-book, is their teacher." Williams comments: "With this act, African American teachers asserted at once that black people were educable, and they demonstrated that some possessed the knowledge required to instruct others."[10]

As soon as the war ended, the organization of learning circles and schools in every conceivable location was spontaneous and widespread: sheds, barns, kitchens, beneath a shady tree by the river. Anyone who learned a little was expected to teach others. Despite the Union victory, White Southerners continued to threaten and use violence against Blacks learning to read. But formerly enslaved people refused to abandon their own interests; they abandoned deference instead and organized themselves for literacy. Northern Whites, missionaries and government officials, were continually amazed, since Black agency confused them. People who had only months earlier gained freedom from the system of chattel slavery contributed whatever money, materials, or labor they could to the building of schoolhouses, even if there was no teacher yet to supervise learning. One invalid, confined to a bed, was carried to a shady spot outdoors where he could teach fifty people, children and adults, how to read. And disputes arose between the Northern Whites and the formerly enslaved Blacks about who was best situated to teach, just as today Teach for America is often challenged by Black communities: "We are better off teaching ourselves" is a powerful rejection of the deference Africans in America have been expected to display toward White benefactors.

Peer-to-peer youth enterprises should be understood as contemporary versions of the "rude and imperfect" cellars, sheds, and corners where Africans in America, immigrants, and Indigenous people try to learn what they will need in order to determine their own futures. Some common agenda, such as the National Student Bill of Rights, will be helpful as an organizing tool to unify the country around a standard of education for democracy. Structures built on false and oppressive calculations of merit will look much less impressive when young people experience viable alternatives to the status quo. With an agenda and an organizing base, these young people can press for changes in the way we educate all children, and more parents will find themselves committed to remaining in the communities where they were raised themselves, able to envision generations learning and thriving there. Once that rootedness becomes plausible, education will be no more problematic than learning to speak one's mother tongue. Children learn to survive in the society they actually live in. Today's society teaches terrible lessons, and young people report as much through their rebellion every day. They also tell us what they need, if we have ears to hear. We can do better. We should.

ACKNOWLEDGMENTS

Thanks to my wife, my sons, and my daughter-in-law, always the richest sources of energy: Diane Kuthy, Matteo Gillen, Eric Lockett, Sammy, Mischa, and Paul Atkinson, and Erin Cunningham. Thanks also to Tom Andrione; Katie Arevalo; Bill and Rick Ayers; Chris Baron; Cortnie Belser; Jason Boone; Mahogany Bosworth; Alanis Brown; Faye Brown; Michaela Brown; Maria Cedillo; Xzavier and Nicole Cheatom; Charnell Covert; Courtland Cox; David Dennis; John Duda; Katherine Engleman; William Engstrand; Ben Forstenzer; Charles Fowler; Peter French; Malcolm Gee; Chris and Asa Goodman; Lawrence Grandpre; Jonothan Gray; Pat Halle; Fernandes Harlee; Mildred Harris; Ralikh Hayes; Gregg Hill; Eberechi (Fred) Ihezie; Adam Jackson; Kevin James; Jamal Jones; Antwain Jordan; David Kandel; Kate Khatib; Iris Kirsch; Andrew Kuthy; Chamir Lawson; Chris Lawson; Jordan Leonard; Dayvon Love; Ellis Marsalis; Ryan Mason; Schanwanda Miller; Marie Mokuba; Rayshon Moore; Chris Moser; Robert, Janet, Maisha, and Omo Moses; Ben Moynihan; Bryant Muldrew; Tre Murphy; Abeni and Bakari Nazeer; Thomas Nikundiwe; Michele Parker; Theresa Perry; Magda Phillips; Terrance Porter; Avis Ransom; Brandon Roane; Ivan Roberts; Betty Garman Robinson; Carla Shalaby; Maryland Shaw; Lester Spence; Victory Swift; Angel Tibbs; Kim Trueheart; Jerell Ward; Maurice Washington; Wayne and Adrian Washington; and the outstanding team at Beacon Press: Helene Atwan, Heidi Bell, Jennifer Canela, Beth Collins, Susan Lumenello, Molly Velazquez-Brown, and my patient editor, Rachael Marks.

NOTES

INTRODUCTION: ORGANIZING, ECONOMICS, AND THE AFRICAN AMERICAN EDUCATIONAL TRADITION

1. Theresa Perry, "Up from the Parched Earth: Toward a Theory of African-American Achievement," in *Young, Gifted, and Black: Promoting High Achievement Among African-American Students*, ed. Theresa Perry, Claude Steele, and Asa G. Hilliard III (Boston: Beacon Press, 2003); Vincent Harding, *There Is a River: The Black Struggle for Freedom in America* (New York: Harcourt Brace and Company, 1981); Vanessa Siddle Walker, *Their Highest Potential: An African American School Community in the Segregated South* (Chapel Hill: University of North Carolina Press, 1996); Heather Andrea Williams, *Self-Taught: African American Education in Slavery and Freedom* (Chapel Hill: University of North Carolina Press, 2005); Charles M. Payne and Carol Sills Strickland, eds., *Teach Freedom: Education for Liberation in the African-American Tradition* (New York: Teachers College Press, 2008); Russell John Rickford, *We Are an African People: Independent Education, Black Power, and the Radical Imagination* (New York: Oxford University Press, 2016).

2. Maryland Department of Juvenile Services, *Data Resource Guide*, 2018, 108, https://djs.state.md.us/Documents/DRG/Data_Resource_Guide _FY2018_full_book.pdf.

3. Coalition for Juvenile Justice, *Deinstitutionalization of Status Offenders (DSO): Facts and Resources* (Washington, DC, May 2011), last revised January 2014, http://www.juvjustice.org/sites/default/files/resource-files /DSO%20Fact%20Sheet%202014.pdf.

4. Jessica Gordon Nembhard, *Collective Courage: A History of African American Cooperative Economic Thought and Practice* (University Park: Penn State University Press, 2014).

5. Joanne Grant, *Ella Baker: Freedom Bound* (New York: John Wiley and Sons, 1998), 8–9.

6. J. Todd Moye, *Ella Baker: Community Organizer of the Civil Rights Movement* (Lanham, MD: Rowman and Littlefield, 2013), 20.

7. Ellen Cantarow, with Susan Gushee O'Malley and Sharon Hartman Strom, *Moving the Mountain: Women Working for Social Change* (Old Westbury, NY: Feminist Press, 1980); Barbara Ransby, *Ella Baker and the Black Freedom Movement: A Radical Democratic Vision* (Chapel Hill: University of North Carolina Press, 2003).

8. Robert P. Moses, "Constitutional Property v. Constitutional People," in *Quality Education as a Constitutional Right: Creating a Grassroots Movement to Transform Public Schools*, ed. Theresa Perry, Robert P. Moses, Joan T. Wynne, Ernesto Cortés Jr., and Lisa Delpit (Boston: Beacon Press, 2010), 82–83.

9. Education and Democracy, *Freedom School Curriculum*, 1964, http://www.educationanddemocracy.org/ED_FSC.html.

CHAPTER 1: FROM CRAWL SPACES TO A YOUTH ECONOMY

1. Perry, "Up from the Parched Earth," 99.

2. Carter G. Woodson, *The Mis-Education of the Negro* ([1933]; n.p.: Seven Treasures Publications, 2010), 23.

3. Omo Moses used the expression "Young people are the power in the room" during a workshop he conducted for the Young People's Project. If memory serves, this was in Los Angeles, 2008.

4. Bernice Johnson Reagon, "Ella's Song," Songtalk Publishing, 1988; Vincent Harding, lecture at United States Social Forum, Detroit, 2010.

5. Leib Sutcher, Linda Darling-Hammond, and Desiree Carver-Thomas, *A Coming Crisis in Teaching? Teacher Supply, Demand, and Shortages in the U.S.* (Palo Alto, CA: Learning Policy Institute, 2016), https://learningpolicyinstitute.org/product/coming-crisis-teaching.

6. Robert P. Moses, conversation with author, 2018.

7. Harding, Social Forum lecture.

8. Robert P. Moses, *Radical Equations: Civil Rights from Mississippi to the Algebra Project* (Boston: Beacon Press, 2001).

9. Ransby, *Ella Baker and the Black Freedom Movement*, 4.

10. Harold A. McDougall, *Black Baltimore: A New Theory of Community* (Philadelphia: Temple University Press, 1993).

11. Patricia Halle, conversation with author, 2016.

12. Dorothy Holland, William S. Lachicotte Jr., Debra Skinner, and Carole Cain, *Identity and Agency in Cultural Worlds* (Cambridge, MA: Harvard University Press, 1998), 52, quoted in Perry, "Up from the Parched Earth," 93.

13. Bettina L. Love, *We Want to Do More Than Survive: Abolitionist Teaching and the Pursuit of Educational Freedom* (Boston: Beacon Press, 2019); Christopher Emdin, *For White Folks Who Teach in the Hood . . . and the Rest of Y'all Too* (Boston: Beacon Press, 2016); Rochelle Gutiérrez, "Living Mathematx: Towards a Vision for the Future," in *Proceedings of the 39th Annual Meeting of the North American Chapter of the International Group for the Psychology of Mathematics Education*, ed. E. Galindo and J. Newton (Indianapolis: Hoosier Association of Mathematics Teacher Educators, 2017), 2–26; Lisa (Leigh) Patel, *Youth Held at the Border: Immigration, Education, and the Politics of Inclusion* (New York: Teachers College Press, 2013).

CHAPTER 2: SOLVING OUR OWN PROBLEMS

1. Etienne Wenger, *Communities of Practice: Learning, Meaning, and Identity* (Cambridge, UK: Cambridge University Press, 1998).
2. M. A. K. Halliday, "Towards a Language-Based Theory of Learning," *Linguistics and Education* 5, no. 2 (1993): 103.
3. See, for example, L. T. Brown et al., "The Rise of Anchor Institutions and the Threat to Community Health: Protecting Community Wealth, Building Community Power," *Kalfou: A Journal of Comparative and Relational Ethnic Studies* 3, no. 1 (2016): 79–100; Antero Pietila, *Not in My Neighborhood: How Bigotry Shaped a Great American City* (Chicago: Ivan R. Dee, 2010).
4. Baltimore City Health Department, "Neighborhood Health Profile Reports," https://health.baltimorecity.gov/neighborhood-health-profile -reports.
5. INCITE! Women of Color Against Violence, eds., *The Revolution Will Not Be Funded: Beyond the Non-Profit Industrial Complex* (Cambridge, MA: South End Press, 2007).
6. For a detailed study of this dynamic, see Thomas Nikundiwe, "(Extra) Ordinary Young People, (Extra)Ordinary Demands: Four Black Men with the Baltimore Algebra Project," PhD diss., Harvard University, 2017.

CHAPTER 3: BUILDING CAPACITY

1. Robert Moses, Mieko Kamii, Susan McAllister Swap, and Jeffrey Howard, "The Algebra Project: Organizing in the Spirit of Ella," *Harvard Educational Review* 59, no. 4 (December 1989): 423–44.

2. Pete Seeger had the excellent idea to sing an often omitted verse of Woody Guthrie's "This Land Is Your Land" during the pre-inauguration concert at the Lincoln Memorial, January 18, 2008, while President-elect Obama listened. The verse mentions a sign saying "Private Property" but only on one side. The other side doesn't say anything, and that's the side that was made for you and me (https://www.youtube.com/watch?v=wnvCPQqQWds).

3. Urban Alliance, *Employment Matters! Strengthening the Youth-To-Work Pipeline Through High-Quality Youth Employment Opportunities*, http://www.theurbanalliance.org/wp-content/uploads/2014/10/UA-Policy-Brief-4.pdf.

4. Virgine Pérotin, *What Do We Really Know About Worker Co-operatives?* (Co-operatives UK, 2016), https://www.uk.coop/sites/default/files/uploads/attachments/worker_co-op_report.pdf; Nina K. Dastur, *Understanding Worker-Owned Cooperatives: A Strategic Guide for Community Organizers* (Center for Community Change, 2012), https://community-wealth.org/sites/clone.community-wealth.org/files/downloads/report-dastur.pdf.

5. Ben Craig and John Pencavel, "The Behavior of Worker Co-operatives: The Plywood Companies of the Pacific Northwest," *American Economic Review* 82, no. 5 (1992): 1083–105; Ben Craig and John Pencavel, "The Objectives of Worker Co-operatives," *Journal of Comparative Economics* 17 (1993): 288–308; Gabriel Burdín and Andrés Dean, "New Evidence on Wages and Employment in Worker Cooperatives Compared with Capitalist Firms," *Journal of Comparative Economics* 37, no. 4 (2009): 517–33; John Pencavel, Luigi Pistaferri, and Fabiano Schivardi, "Wages, Employment, and Capital in Capitalist and Worker-Owned Firms," *Industrial and Labor Relations Review*, 60, no. 1 (2006): 23–44.

6. This is not inevitable. Even in cooperative organizations, the efforts of strong or assertive individuals or traditions of deference to an authority often result in the collective's acquiescence to centralized or hierarchical decisions. Worker cooperatives can sometimes settle into certain familial patterns, deferring to a strong leader as family members defer to a strong matriarch or patriarch. The members of such a cooperative are bound by love, respect, and sharing of resources, but the political structure is autocratic rather than democratic. Worker cooperatives can also evolve toward more traditional capitalist styles, where decision-making is also centralized but relations are less loving, more alienated, and tend toward material and social inequalities. This is certainly a danger in the

specific context of the United States today, since the broader political economy, of course, displays and validates these tendencies.

7. Lawrence Goodwyn, *The Populist Moment: A Short History of the Agrarian Revolt in America* (Oxford, UK: Oxford University Press, 1978), 1.

8. Melva Grant et al., "Polynomial Calculus: Rethinking the Role of Calculus in High Schools," workshop and sharing group, *Proceedings of the International Congress on Mathematics Education-12* (Seoul, South Korea, July 2012), 7294–302, https://www.researchgate.net/publication /264383804_Polynomial_calculus_rethinking_the_role_of_calculus _in_high_schools.

9. "Use the Power of Youth to Solve Social Problems: Yunus," *Daily Star* (Dhaka, Bangladesh), May 29, 2015, https://www.thedailystar.net/busi ness/use-the-power-youth-solve-social-problems-yunus-89020.

10. INCITE! Women of Color Against Violence, *The Revolution Will Not Be Funded.*

11. Antwain Jordan, codirector of the Baltimore Algebra Project, in conversation with author, 2015.

CHAPTER 4: AN EDUCATIONAL BUREAUCRACY BUILT ON VIOLENCE

1. I am judging from the photos in the Stuyvesant High School yearbook, 1944. Algebra Project founder Bob Moses graduated from Stuyvesant in 1952 and remembers only one other African American classmate, the psychiatrist Alvin Poussaint.

2. Corrie Schoenberg, *Calculated Choices: Equity and Opportunity in Baltimore City Public Schools* (Baltimore: Fund for Educational Excellence, 2017), https://ffee.org/wp-content/uploads/Calculated-Choices-Final -Report.pdf.

3. Rachel E. Durham and Erik Westlund, *A Descriptive Look at College Enrollment and Degree Completion of Baltimore City Graduates* (Baltimore: Baltimore Education Research Consortium, 2011), http:// baltimore-berc.org/pdfs/CollegeEnrollmentFull.pdf.

4. Benjamin F. Evans, Emily Zimmerman, Steven H. Woolf, Amber D. Haley, *Neighborhood Characteristics and Health in Baltimore, Maryland* (Richmond: Center on Human Needs, Virginia Commonwealth University, 2012).

5. "Israel: New Laws Marginalize Palestinian Arab Citizens," Human Rights Watch, March 20, 2011, http://www.hrw.org/news/2011/03/30

/israel-new-laws-marginalize-palestinian-arab-citizens, quoted in Ali Abunimah, *The Battle for Justice in Palestine* (Chicago: Haymarket, 2014), 29.

6. Primo Levi, *If This Is a Man*, in *The Complete Works of Primo Levi*, vol. 1, ed. Ann Goldstein, trans. Stuart Woolf (New York: Liveright Publishing Corporation, 2015), 123–24.

7. David Stovall, "Are We Ready for 'School' Abolition? Thoughts and Practices of Radical Imaginary in Education," *Taboo: The Journal of Culture and Education* 17, no. 1 (Winter 2018), https://doi.org/10.31390/taboo.17.1.06.

8. Phillip Lovell and Julia Isaacs, *The Impact of the Mortgage Crisis on Children and Their Education* (Washington, DC: First Focus, 2008), https://www.brookings.edu/wp-content/uploads/2016/06/04_mortgage_crisis_isaacs.pdf.

9. Michel Martin and Brian Poe, "Mother Jailed for School Fraud, Flares Controversy," National Public Radio, January 28, 2011, https://www.npr.org/2011/01/28/133306180/Mother-Jailed-For-School-Fraud-Flares-Controversy.

10. Even this obvious point is blurry in America. President Obama did not meet at the White House with just any of the thousands of Black Americans arrested without cause each year. He met with Henry Louis Gates Jr., a Harvard professor, not because of the professor's humanity but because of his status. What other logic could explain why the president never met with the unemployed teenagers in Baltimore described in his Justice Department's own report as unjustly detained and strip-searched on public streets in front of their own homes?

11. Claude McKay, "If We Must Die," *Liberator* 2, no. 7 (July 1919): 21.

12. Charles Cobb, *This Nonviolent Stuff'll Get You Killed: How Guns Made the Civil Rights Movement Possible* (New York: Basic Books, 2014).

13. Thomas Nikundiwe, conversation with author, 2017.

14. Lester K. Spence, *Knocking the Hustle: Against the Neoliberal Turn in Black Politics* (Brooklyn, NY: Punctum Books, 2015). See also Woodson, *The Mis-Education of the Negro*.

15. Leo Tolstoy, *War and Peace*, trans. Ann Dunnigan (New York: Signet Classics, 1968), 1432.

16. Charles M. Payne, *So Much Reform, So Little Change: The Persistence of Failure in Urban Schools* (Cambridge, MA: Harvard Education Press, 2008).

17. Tolstoy, *War and Peace*, 1435.

18. Needless to say, the structure of military command is intimately connected to patriarchal oppression.
19. Thomas S. Kuhn, *The Structure of Scientific Revolutions*, 50th anniversary ed. (1962; Chicago: University of Chicago Press, 2012).

CHAPTER 5: BASE COMMUNITIES

1. The work of Shawn Ginwright thoroughly documents this effect; see, for example, *Black Youth Rising: Activism and Radical Healing in Urban America* (New York: Teachers College Press, 2010).
2. From Charles Cobb's description of the effect of the 1964 Freedom Schools in Mississippi, conversation with author, 2014.
3. McDougall, *Black Baltimore*. I am grateful to Lawrence Grandpre of Leaders of a Beautiful Struggle for referring me to this source.
4. Gray died April 19, 2015, from spinal cord injuries sustained during an arrest and subsequent "rough ride" in a police van. Six police officers were charged for the murder, but none was convicted.
5. McDougall, *Black Baltimore*, 21.
6. McDougall, *Black Baltimore*, 161.
7. Moses, *Radical Equations*.
8. McDougall, *Black Baltimore*, 20.
9. Other traditions are available too. See, for example, Rochelle Gutiérrez's discussion of In Lak'ech, reciprocity, and Nepantla in her "Living Mathematx: Towards a Vision for the Future," 2–26.
10. Official Kwanzaa Web Site, http://www.officialkwanzaawebsite.org /NguzoSaba.shtml, accessed March 22, 2019.
11. Mindy Thompson Fullilove, *Root Shock: How Tearing Up City Neighborhoods Hurts America, and What We Can Do About It* (New York: Ballantine, 2004).
12. Moses, *Radical Equations*.
13. An observation sentence is a sentence whose truth-value can be agreed upon by any observers present at an event. For example, if we are at a bus stop, "A girl is sitting on the bench" is an observation sentence, since anyone observing can determine whether the sentence is true or false. "A girl is waiting for the bus" is not an observation sentence, because observers cannot determine the girl's purpose just by looking at her. She may have just gotten off a bus and paused to think for a minute before heading home (example from the Algebra Project Curriculum, www.algebra.org).

14. See my description in *Educating for Insurgency* of learning how *Brown v. Board* desegregated public education while sitting in an all-Black or all-Brown public school classroom; Jay Gillen, *Educating for Insurgency: The Roles of Young People in Schools of Poverty* (Oakland: AK Press, 2014), part 2.
15. Ralph Ellison, *Shadow and Act* (New York: Vintage, 1964).
16. Handcuffed defendants in Baltimore's courtrooms are routinely instructed by judges or bailiffs to raise their right hand and swear to tell the truth. Recognizing that the instruction, "raise your right hand," is impossible to execute given that the defendants' hands are cuffed together behind their backs, the judges mutter "as best you can" to acknowledge the absurdity of the instruction. Can the language of courts be taken at face value? What does it hide? What would have to change for the language of courts to become trustworthy?
17. Christopher Emdin, urging teachers to learn from students of color by "sitting down and listening," calls respectability "the enemy of progressive education" (lecture, Loyola University, Baltimore, 2018).
18. See Lisa Delpit and Joanne Kilgour Dowdy, eds., *The Skin That We Speak: Thoughts on Language and Culture in the Classroom* (New York: New Press, 2002).
19. Pierre Bourdieu and Jean-Claude Passeron, *Reproduction in Education, Society and Culture*, trans. Richard Nice (London: Sage Publications, 1977), 42.
20. Talila Lewis (keynote address, Free Minds, Free People Conference, Baltimore, 2017) encouraged education activists to always include people with disabilities in any naming of a population, e.g., "race, class, gender, immigration status, sexual orientation . . . and disability."
21. Lewis, keynote address.
22. Lester Spence and Son of Nun (Kevin James) both spoke about mental health issues at the 2640 Space, Baltimore, October 19, 2017.
23. Carol Dashiff, Wendy DiMicco, Beverly Myers, and Kathy Sheppard, "Poverty and Adolescent Mental Health," *Journal of Child and Adolescent Psychiatric Nursing* 22, no. 1 (2009): 23–32, https://onlinelibrary.wiley.com/doi/full/10.1111/j.1744-6171.2008.00166.x.
24. "I'm Determined: Empowering Self-Determined Behavior," Virginia Department of Education, http:www.imdetermined.org.
25. Ella Baker, 1969 speech, quoted in Moses, *Radical Equations*, 3.

NOTES | **183**

CHAPTER 6: ACCOUNTABILITY, THE NATIONAL STUDENT BILL OF RIGHTS, AND THE LEGACY OF STRUGGLE

1. The word "grade" does not yet appear in Samuel Johnson's 1755 dictionary. Before the eighteenth century, the *Oxford English Dictionary* includes a definition for "grade" meaning a step in a staircase, but "grade" to indicate a performance in school does not appear until the early nineteenth century, when the industrial revolution is already well underway. Thom Hartmann suggests that the practice of paying teachers by the student was taken over from piece-work payment systems in manufacturing, and lent itself to quantification of student results, i.e., grading (*Thom Hartmann's Complete Guide to ADHD: Help for Your Family at Home, School & Work* [Nevada City, CA: Underwood Books, 2000]). The rise of "Taylorism" or "scientific management" in the nineteenth and early twentieth centuries coincides with the use of percentages to standardize measurement of academic performance. In 1911, Max Meyer writes, "The grade has in more than one sense a cash value, and if there is no uniformity of grading in an institution, this means directly that values are stolen from some and undeservedly presented to others" ("Experiences with the Grading System of the University of Missouri," *Science* 33, no. 852 [1911]: 661). Jack Schneider and Ethan Hutt discuss Meyer's analysis in "Making the Grade: A History of the A–F Marking Scheme," *Journal of Curriculum Studies* 46, no. 2 (2014), http://dx.doi .org/10.1080/00220272.2013.790480. See also Kenneth Gray, "Why We Will Lose: Taylorism in America's High Schools," *Phi Delta Kappan* 74, no. 5 (January 1993): 370–74, https://www.jstor.org/stable/20404887 ?seq=1#metadata_info_tab_contents.

2. Other versions of a Student Bill of Rights have been developed elsewhere, notably in Milwaukee, Providence, and the state of California.

3. National Student Bill of Rights Task Force, National Student Bill of Rights for All Youth, https://nationalstudentbillofrights.wordpress.com /the-rights-we-should-have, accessed March 27, 2019.

4. A similar lesson has been learned all over the world in the last one hundred years as women have gained access to formal political and economic roles. Productivity, wealth, and education increase everywhere that women move toward social and political equality.

5. Moses, "Constitutional Property" discusses this issue in detail.

6. Raynard Sanders, "The New Orleans Public Education Experiment: Children Lose—Education Reformers Win," in *Twenty-First-Century*

Jim Crow Schools: The Impact of Charters on Public Education, ed. Raynard Sanders, David Stovall, and Terrenda White (Boston: Beacon, 2018), 15–17.

7. Goodwin Liu, "Education, Equality, and National Citizenship," *Yale Law Journal* 116 (2006), http://digitalcommons.law.yale.edu/ylj/vol116/iss2/2.

8. M. K. Asante, "Racism, Consciousness, and Afrocentricity," in Gerald Early, ed., *Lure and Loathing: Essays on Race, Identity, and the Ambivalence of Assimilation* (New York: Penguin Books, 1993), 127–43.

9. Moses points out that there could not have been any "papers" in 1787 to credential citizens, because the nation was still in the process of being established. In all senses, the Founders were undocumented immigrants.

10. Williams, *Self-Taught*.